LETTERING & TYPE

The works of commercial sign painters often showcase inventive and accomplished examples of custom lettering in use.

LETTERING & TYPE

CREATING LETTERS AND DESIGNING TYPEFACES

BRUCE WILLEN   NOLEN STRALS

WITH A FOREWORD BY ELLEN LUPTON

PRINCETON ARCHITECTURAL PRESS, NEW YORK

Published by
Princeton Architectural Press
37 East Seventh Street
New York, New York 10003

For a free catalog of books, call 1.800.722.6657.
Visit our website at www.papress.com.

Library of Congress Cataloging-in-Publication Data
Willen, Bruce, 1981–
Lettering & type : creating letters and designing typefaces / Bruce Willen
and Nolen Strals ; with a foreword by Ellen Lupton. — 1st ed.
129 p. : ill. (some col.) ; 22 cm. — (Design briefs)
Includes index.
Includes bibliographical references.
ISBN 978-1-56898-765-1 (alk. paper)
1. Type and type-founding. 2. Lettering. 3. Graphic design (Typography)
I. Strals, Nolen, 1978– II. Title. III. Title: Lettering and type.
Z250.W598 2009
686.2'24—dc22
                                        2009003470

PROJECT EDITOR: Clare Jacobson

COPY EDITOR: Zipporah W. Collins

DESIGNER: Post Typography

ADDITIONAL DESIGNERS: Sara Frantzman and Eric Karnes

PRIMARY TYPEFACES: Dolly and Auto, both designed by Underware

SPECIAL THANKS TO: Nettie Aljian, Bree Anne Apperley, Sara
Bader, Nicola Bednarek, Janet Behning, Becca Casbon, Carina Cha,
Penny (Yuen Pik) Chu, Carolyn Deuschle, Russell Fernandez, Pete
Fitzpatrick, Wendy Fuller, Jan Haux, Aileen Kwun, Nancy Eklund
Later, Linda Lee, Laurie Manfra, John Myers, Katharine Myers,
Lauren Nelson Packard, Dan Simon, Andrew Stepanian, Jennifer
Thompson, Paul Wagner, Joseph Weston, and Deb Wood of Princeton
Architectural Press —Kevin C. Lippert, publisher

CONTENTS

FOREWORD

ELLEN LUPTON

Letters are the throbbing heart of visual communication. For all the talk of the death of print and the dominance of the image, written words remain the engine of information exchange. Text is everywhere. It is a medium and a message. It is a noun and a verb. As design becomes a more widespread and open-source practice, typography has emerged as a powerful creative tool for writers, artists, makers, illustrators, and activists as well as for graphic designers. Mastering the art of arranging letters in space and time is essential knowledge for anyone who crafts communications for page or screen.

This book goes beyond the basics of typographic arrangement (line length, line spacing, column structure, page layout, etc.) to focus on the form and construction of letters themselves. While typography uses standardized letterforms, the older arts of lettering and handwriting consist of unique forms made with a variety of tools. Today, the applications and potential of lettering and type are broader than ever before, as designers create handmade letterforms, experimental alphabets, and sixteenth-century typeface revivals with equal confidence.

Type design is a hugely complex and specialized discipline. To do it well demands deep immersion in the technical, legal, and economic standards of the type business as well as formidable drawing skills and a firm grasp of history. This book provides a friendly, openhearted introduction to this potentially intimidating field, offering a way into not only the vocabulary and techniques of font design but also the sister arts of lettering, handwriting, calligraphy, and logo design. Simple, inventive exercises expose readers to creative methods, inviting them to explore fresh ways to understand, create, and combine forms. Throughout the book, the voices of some of the world's leading type and lettering artists illuminate the creative process.

Authors Bruce Willen and Nolen Strals are two of the sharpest young minds on the contemporary design scene. I first met them as my students at Maryland Institute College of Art (MICA), where they now teach courses in experimental typography and lettering. Even as students, they were never march-in-line designers. Instead, they were intellectuals with an iconoclastic edge who pursued their own view of art and design, connected with music and cultural activism more than with the standard professional discourse. Along with their maverick spirit, Bruce and Nolen have always

**Saks Fifth Avenue
Valentine**
Lettering, 2008
Marian Bantjes
*Words communicate both visual
and written information. These
letters' ornate flourishes eclipse
the words themselves to form a
larger image.*

brought an incisive and controlled intelligence to their work, which today ranges from hand-screened, hand-lettered posters for the Baltimore music scene to sophisticated graphics for the *New York Times* and the U.S. Green Building Council.

The initial concept and outline for this book were developed in collaboration with MICA's Center for Design Thinking, which works with its students and faculty to develop and disseminate design research. The book's voice and philosophy reflect the authors' unique point of view as artists and thinkers. Letters, they suggest, are alive and kicking. Anyone who is fueled with a dose of desire and an ounce of courage is invited to plunge in and take on twenty-six of the world's most infamous and influential characters. The language of letters ranges from the übersophistication of fonts designed for books to the singular quirks of custom logotypes and the clandestine mysteries of graffiti. It's all there to be explored and grappled with. Anyone who tries a hand at designing letters will walk away with—at the very least—a deepened respect for the opponent.

PREFACE

Practical information about creating letters and type often amounts to a series of truisms or guidelines for executing a particular process or style. While a designer can apply every "rule" or typographic axiom literally, what makes lettering and type design endlessly fascinating is the flexibility to interpret and sometimes even break these rules. *Lettering & Type* aims to present devotees and students of letters with the background to implement critical lettering and type design principles, discarding them when appropriate, and to offer readers a framework for understanding and approaching their own work—not only the "how" but also the "where," "when," and "why" of the alphabet.

Part of our own fascination with letters comes from the endlessly surprising nature of these common objects. The ubiquity of letters in our daily lives makes them a familiar subject matter, ready to be interpreted by generations of designers, artists, and bored schoolchildren alike. Like many other designers, we have loved letters from an early age, inventing our own comic book sound effects, illustrating our names in our notebooks, and drawing rock band logos on our desks during math class. We have yet to outgrow the enjoyment of losing ourselves inside a lettering or type project. In a world governed by increasingly short deadlines, instant communications, and machines that let us do more with less, spending an entire day drawing a handful of letters is indeed a beautiful and luxurious act.

In *Lettering & Type* we have sought to create a book with a wide focus on both the methods and the reasons for making letters, something that will appeal to students of type design, fine artists, graphic designers, letterers, and anyone else with a curiosity about the forms and functions of the alphabet. Our approach to *Lettering & Type* comes from our experience teaching at the Maryland Institute College of Art, as well as our own practice, which often extends into graphic design, illustration, lettering, and type design. We have augmented our firsthand knowledge with the inspiring work of contemporary designers and artists, and with lessons absorbed from a wide range of theorists and historians.

Compliments of the B&O Railroad Company
Dinner menu, 1884
Letters and design respond to new ideas and technologies. This illustration and its electric lettering herald a newly connected world, accessible by the telegraph and railroad.
Library of Congress, Rare Book and Special Collections Division.

Geometric Alphabet
Book cover (detail), 1930
William Addison Dwiggins
*Parallel to similar explorations
in modern art and architecture,
lettering and type creations by
many early-twentieth-century
designers celebrated geometric
and mechanical shapes.*

Opposite:
B vs RUCE
Drawing by the author, age ten.

Lettering & Type is organized into four sections, which build a broad, theoretical overview of lettering, typography, and the roman alphabet into a many-bladed reference tool for designing letters and typefaces.

Section One, "Context," investigates the ideas and history that inform lettering and typography, exploring the concepts of legibility, context, and creativity while illuminating the alphabet's complex evolution. This intellectual and historical context sets the stage for Section Two, "Systems & Type-ologies," which discusses the systems underlying every typeface or lettering treatment and outlines a framework for approaching, analyzing, and creating the attributes and elements of lettering and type. Section Three, "Creating Letters," dives deeper into the realities of constructing letterforms, expanding the theoretical approach into a practical discussion of specific methods and styles. Section Four, "Making Letters Work," looks at letters as they are applied—in situations from type design, logos, and lettering treatments to psyche-delic posters and fantastic illustrative alphabets—providing a practical and inclusive foundation for designing typefaces and implementing lettering in the real world.

Accompanying the concepts discussed in the text, many contemporary and historical examples of typefaces, graphic design, and lettering appear throughout *Lettering & Type*. Supporting these illustrations are diagrams and exercises meant to expand on specific ideas while dispensing lessons and advice that can be applied to the reader's own work. Interviews with skilled practitioners in the fields of type design, lettering, fine art, and graphic design present contemporary perspectives and approaches to designing and working with letters.

Envisioning, writing, and assembling all of these elements to create *Lettering & Type* has been an enlightening and energizing process for us, as we have immersed ourselves in the history and minutiae of lettering and type design. We hope that readers will find similar insight and inspiration within these pages, no matter what their relationship is to the alphabet.

ACKNOWLEDGMENTS

Lettering & Type would not have been possible without the generosity of the design community and of this volume's many contributors. We dedicate *Lettering & Type* to everyone who has contributed artwork, wisdom, and editorial suggestions, and those who have supported us along the way. In particular we thank Ellen Lupton for her confidence in our abilities and her constant encouragement and guidance in many of our creative endeavors. Her extraordinary *Thinking with Type* was the inspiration and exemplar for this volume and sets a high benchmark for every typography treatise that follows it.

In addition we wish to the thank the following people whose contributions, guidance, and assistance have helped us realize *Lettering & Type*: Clare Jacobson at Princeton Architectural Press and copy editor Zipporah Collins, whose incisive guidance and editing have brought this project to fruition; Ken Barber, Ryan Brown, John Buchtel, Lincoln Cushing, Jennifer Daniel, Cara Di Edwardo, John Downer, Mike Essl, Shaun Flynn, Brendan Fowler, Sara Frantzman, Laura Gencarella, Sara Gerrish, Isaac Gertman, Sibylle Hagmann, Nancy Harris Roeumy, Kathryn Hodson, Chris Jackson, Denis Kitchen, Tal Leming, Barry McGee, Matt Porterfield, Christian Schwartz, Underware, Kyle Van Horn, Armin Vit, as well as all our other friends, family, supporters, clients, and collaborators throughout the years, including our former instructors and current colleagues at the Maryland Institute College of Art and the supportive MICA community at large, and especially our students—who have in turn educated us—and whose work graces these pages.

Most deeply of all we thank Sarah Templin and Sara Tomko (for their enormous patience and tireless support), Richard and Margaret Willen (for the invaluable advice and editing), Katie Strals, Pete and Lou Strals, Chris Strals, Mema, Papa, Grandma, all the Willens, Cohens, Needles, and Moores, and all the Browns, Mumms, and Carlowes.

Main Drag
Installation, 2001
Margaret Kilgallen
Photo courtesy of Barry McGee

CONTEXT

LEGIBILITY, CONTEXT, AND CREATIVITY

Letters and the words that they form are homes for language and ideas. Like buildings, letterforms reflect the climate and the cultural environment for which they are designed while adopting the personality of their content and designers. Although letters are inherently functional, their appearance can evoke a surprisingly wide range of emotions and associations—everything from formality and professionalism to playfulness, sophistication, crudeness, and beyond. Designers and letterers balance such contextual associations with the alphabet's functional nature, melding the concerns of legibility and context with their own creative voices.

As in all applied arts, functionality lies at the heart of lettering and typography. Legibility is what makes letterforms recognizable and gives an alphabet letter the ability and power to speak through its shape. Just as the distinction between a building and a large outdoor sculpture is occasionally blurred, a written or printed character can be only so far removed from its legible form before it becomes merely a confluence of lines in space. Legible letters look like themselves and will not be mistaken for other letters or shapes—an A that no longer looks like an A ceases to function.

Letters or words whose visual form confuses or overwhelms the viewer disrupt communication and diminish their own functionality. Such disruptions are generally undesirable, but the acceptable level of legibility varies according to context. Some letterers and designers pursue an idea or visual style rather than straightforward utility. In these cases, the appearance of the letters themselves can take on as much importance as the text they contain or even more. When used appropriately, less legible letterforms ask the reader to spend time with their shapes and to become a more active participant in the reading process. Unusual, illustrative, or otherwise hard-to-read letters often convey a highly specific visual or intellectual tone and are meant to be looked at rather than through.

Letter Box Kites
Alphabet, 2008
Andrew Byrom
The letters of the alphabet do not always exist in two dimensions. Letters can be structural, functional, time-based, or even interactive.

Laptop for Sale
Photocopied flyer, 2008
Rowen Frazer
This flyer plays with context through a tongue-in-cheek, hand-drawn interpretation of pixel lettering.

Opposite top:
Les Yeux Sans Visage
T-shirt graphic and typeface, 2006
Wyeth Hansen
Hansen's typeface, Didon't, pushes the high-contrast forms of eighteenth-century modern type to their natural extreme. Despite the disappearance of the letters' thin strokes, the characters' underlying forms can still be discerned.

Unlike contemporary art's voracious quest for new forms, the impetus to create unconventional or groundbreaking letters is generally less urgent to type designers and letterers, whose subject matter is based on thousands of years of historical precedent. As a letterform becomes more radical or unorthodox, it begins to lose its legibility and usefulness, requiring designers to balance the new with the familiar. This has not prevented letterers, artists, and designers from creating an endless variety of novel and experimental alphabets. New forms and experiments slowly widen the spectrum of legibility, shifting and expanding the vocabulary of letters.

Two thousand years of reading and writing the roman alphabet have shaped the standards of legibility and continue to sculpt it today. What was regarded as a clear and beautiful writing style for a twelfth-century Gothic manuscript is to today's readers as difficult to decipher as a tortuous graffiti script. Nineteenth-century typographers considered sans serif typefaces crude and hard to read, yet these faces are ubiquitous and widely accepted in the twenty-first century. Familiarity and usage define what readers consider legible.

The tastes and history that inform legibility are part of the context in which letters live and work. Often hidden but always present, context comprises the what, where, when, who, and how of lettering and type. At its most basic, context relates to the ultimate use of any letter: What message will the letterforms communicate? Where and when will they appear? How will they be reproduced? Who will view them? But context also represents the broader cultural and social environment in which letters function. Nothing is more important to an artist or designer than context, because it provides the structure from which to learn and work.

Centuries of baggage have colored different styles of letters with a wide array of associations, as contextual relationships are continually forged and forgotten. When creating and using letterforms, designers harness, reinforce, and invent these social and cultural associations. Long before the development of movable type, the stately capital lettering styles of the Romans stood for power, learning, and sophistication. As early as the ninth century, scholars, artists, and politicians associated these qualities with Imperial Rome and sought to invoke them by adopting Roman lettering styles. Even today, graphic designers employ typefaces such as Trajan, based on Roman capitals, to convey an air of classical

Swiss
HELVETICA, 1957, Max Miedinger

Gruyère
BLUR, 1992, Neville Brody

Emmentaler
TRACE, 2008, COMA

Schabziger
BROADCLOTH, 2005, Post Typography

Tilsiter
POST-BITMAP SCRIPTER HELVETICA, 2004, Jonathan Keller

Raclette
THE CLASH, 2006, COMA

MUTSCHLI
HELVETICA DRAWN FROM MEMORY, 2006, Mike Essl

Appenzeller
SIGNIFFICIENT, 2007, Jonathan Keller

These fonts all take the typeface Helvetica as their point of departure. By redrawing, distorting, or digitally reprogramming its letterforms, the designers reinterpret this ubiquitous font in new ways.

The individuality of hand lettering can allow the artist's drawing style to act as a visual signature. Both of these posters are cohesive despite their assortments of disparate letterforms.

Practice and Preach
Poster, 2004
Ed Fella

Hotdogs and Rocket Fuel
Poster, 2007
Jonny Hannah

sophistication. Similarly, the crude stencil lettering painted on industrial and military equipment now appears on T-shirts, advertisements, and posters where the designer wishes to present a rough and rugged image. Even the most isolated or academically constrained letterforms inevitably evoke cultural and historical associations.

Letters' connotations and contextual relationships shift over time. Unexpected usage of a specific style of type or lettering can create an entirely new set of associations—psychedelic artists of the 1960s co-opted nineteenth-century ornamental type styles as a symbol of the counterculture. More routinely, the connotations of fonts change through hundreds of small blows over the years. Type styles like Bodoni, which were considered revolutionary and difficult to read when first introduced, are today used to imply elegance and traditionalism. Likewise, the degraded lettering of the underground punk culture in the 1970s and 1980s is now associated with the corporate marketing of soft drinks, sneakers, and skateboards.

While these contextual relationships often suggest a specific style or approach to a lettering problem, the unlimited possibilities of lettering and type accommodate numerous individual interpretations. Even subtle changes to the appearance of letters can alter the content's voice. Designers sometimes add new perspectives or layers of meaning by introducing an unexpected approach or contrast. Lettering a birth announcement as if it were a horror movie poster might not seem entirely appropriate, but, depending on how seriously the new parents take themselves, it may express the simultaneous joy and terror of birth and child rearing. The voice of the designer or letterer, whether loud or soft, can add as much to a text as its content or author. The designer's ability to interpret context and address legibility underlies the creative success and the ultimate soul of lettering and type.

Individual artists and designers inject creativity into the process of making letters through their concept, approach, and personal style. Sometimes this individuality takes a very visible form: an artist's emblematic handwriting or lettering technique acts as a unifying visual voice to words or letterforms. More frequently, a particular idea or discovery informs creative type and lettering: a type designer stumbles upon an especially well-matched system of shapes for a new typeface, or a letterer adds a subtle-yet-decisive embellishment to a word.

Despite the countless numbers of letterforms that have been written, designed, and printed, the possibilities of the roman alphabet have yet to be exhausted. The skills, motives, and knowledge of letterers and type designers continue to influence the way that text is understood and perceived, placing the creation of letters within both visual and intellectual spheres. The designer's ability to balance and control legibility, context, and creativity is the power to shape the written word.

The letters of the roman alphabet have adopted many forms and styles over several millennia. These are just some of the common variants of the letter A.

A COMPRESSED HISTORY OF THE ROMAN ALPHABET

As tools and symbols that exist at the nexus of art, commerce, and ideas, letters reflect the same cultural forces that inform all other aspects of society. Institutions and authorities from the Catholic Church to the Bauhaus to the Metropolitan Transportation Authority have used their political and cultural clout to influence, manipulate, and establish the alphabet's prevailing forms. Letters are not created in a vacuum, and their appearance is as subject to the whims of power and taste as any other feature of society. The roman alphabet's history cannot be separated from the history of Western civilization.

The shapes of the alphabet as we recognize them today became standardized and codified in the fifteenth century. Working during a period of commercial expansion and technological innovation, Renaissance typographers took handwriting and lettering styles and systematized them into movable type, a set of elements that could be rearranged and reproduced. Type had already been in use for centuries in China,[1] but the compact and efficient character set of the roman alphabet made it especially adaptable to printing. This powerful combination would spread the alphabet and literacy across the Western Hemisphere.

The roman alphabet's phonetic nature makes it ideally suited to typography. Where Chinese languages employ a logographic alphabet comprising tens of thousands of distinct characters, the roman alphabet consists of twenty-six easy-to-learn letters and their variants. Each letter corresponds to specific sounds of speech. Though not perfectly phonetic—some phonemes are conveyed through combinations like th, and many letters represent multiple sounds—the roman alphabet is a potent system for transcribing written language. The ancient Greeks, whose own writing system eventually cross-pollinated with the Romans', referred to the alphabet as *stoicheia* (elements), in recognition of its powerful and fundamental nature.[2]

Greece adapted its written alphabet from Phoenicia's, conforming Phoenician characters to the Greek language. This early Greek writing system filtered through the Etruscan civilization to the Romans, who refined and codified it to such a degree that the Roman alphabet influenced later evolutions of Greek. By the first century AD, the Roman uppercase was fully developed, and its forms are documented in the formal inscriptions carved on edifices throughout the Roman Empire. This ancient

1. Robert Bringhurst, *The Elements of Typographic Style*, version 2.5 (Point Roberts, WA: Hartley and Marks, 2002), 119.

2. Johanna Drucker, *The Alphabetic Labyrinth: The Letters in History and Imagination* (New York: Thames and Hudson, 1999).

Opposite:
Lindisfarne Gospels, Saint Mark's Gospel opening
Illuminated manuscript, 710–721
Eadfrith, Bishop of Lindisfarne
Insular medieval artists in the British Isles departed from the Roman forms of the alphabet, creating inventive and highly decorative letterforms such as the "INI" that dominates this incipit page.
© The British Library Board. All Rights Reserved. Cotton Nero D. IV, f.95. British Library, London.

Roman alphabet is a direct ancestor of contemporary letterforms, and its composition appears surprisingly similar to our own roman uppercase. The term *capital letters* even derives from the location of inscriptions on Roman monuments, where this style of letter is typically found.

Unlike the uppercase alphabet, which has clear origins, the roman lowercase has a more convoluted background. The Romans considered their inscriptional, uppercase alphabet a form and style distinct from their informal writing scripts and cursives. Carefully built from multiple strokes of the chisel or brush, the stately Roman capitals are lettering, as opposed to the handwriting used for books and legal documents. Just as contemporary designers choose specific fonts for different situations, the Romans chose divergent styles and even different artisans for each unique application. Contemporary roman uppercase comes from lettering, while the roman lowercase forms are based on handwriting.

As Christianity became a dominant force in the Roman Empire, the church deliberately began to distinguish its writing and lettering from the styles it associated with Rome's pagan past. Greek—which was the church's official language—and its lettering influenced early Christian inscriptions, adding more freedom and looseness to the Romans' balanced alphabet. Emperor Constantine gave his blessing to a writing style called *uncial*, which became the standard hand for many Christian texts. These Greco-Christian influences from within the empire collided with the writing styles and runic forms of invading northern European tribes, who by the fifth century had overrun Rome several times.

The years after the fall of the Roman Empire were a turbulent time for Europe and for the alphabet. Such periods of social, political, and technological upheaval

A Rough Timeline of the Roman Alphabet

The alphabet's evolution is not linear. Divergent styles, schools, and practices have coexisted and overlapped throughout the history of the roman alphabet. This timeline loosely traces the history of some styles and movements that are key to the evolution of the alphabet. Many of these writing, lettering, and typography styles correspond with important historical trends, reflecting the external forces that shape the alphabet's prevailing forms.

300 B.C.	200 B.C.	100 B.C.

GREEK

FORMAL GREEK ALPHABET

Classical Ionic/eastern alphabet adopted and used in Athens.

ROMAN ALPHABET

Early formal lettering styles, as preserved on Roman inscriptions.

often correspond with challenges and revisions to social and artistic standards—the Industrial Revolution, the years between the two world wars, and the development of the personal computer all correspond to fertile and experimental periods in lettering and typography. The early Middle Ages were no exception, as a wide variety of new lettering styles and alphabets proliferated in Europe. Since the central authority and influence of Rome had dissolved, an increasing number of regional variations on the alphabet developed around local influences, Christian writing styles, and the angular letterforms of northern Europe.

During this time, monks and scribes kept alive the basic structure of the roman alphabet through the copying of manuscripts and books, including Greek, Roman, and especially Christian texts. Some of these source manuscripts contained ornamental initial capitals at the beginnings of pages or verses. As monks transcribed the words of the gospels and manuscripts, they began, particularly in the British Isles, to create extravagantly embellished initials and title pages whose lettering owed little to the Roman tradition. These Insular artists treated letters abstractly, distorting and outlining their forms to fill them with color, pattern, and imagery. Some of the wildly inventive shapes are more decorative than legible—these pages were meant to be looked at more than read. The clergy, who already knew the gospel openings by heart, and a predominantly illiterate society could view the exquisite lettering of these incipit (opening) pages as visual manifestations of God's word.

The wide variety of highly personalized, decorative, and irregular letters that proliferated during these years reflect Europe's fractured and isolated political environment. In 800 AD, Charlemagne briefly reunited western Europe under the banner of the Holy Roman Emperor. Consciously invoking Imperial Rome,

For more on the evolution of the roman alphabet and typography, see Nicolete Gray, A History of Lettering (Oxford: Phaidon Press, 1986); Johanna Drucker, The Alphabetic Labyrinth (New York: Thames and Hudson, 1999); Gerrit Noordzij, Letterletter (Point Roberts, WA: Hartley and Marks, 2000); and Harry Carter, A View of Early Typography (London: Hyphen Press, 2002).

100 A.D.	200	300

ROMAN

CLASSICAL ROMAN LETTERING

Formal Roman alphabet fully developed and in use, as exemplified by the inscription on Trajan's Column in Rome.

ROMAN RUSTICS

Quicker, slightly less formal styles than Trajan letters— typically written with a pen or brush.

OLD ROMAN CURSIVE

An early script used for informal writing.

Gothic lettering, c. 1497
Giacomo Filippo Foresti
Sharp, pen-drawn gothic lettering was used throughout Europe in the late Middle Ages. Writing and lettering styles such as Rotunda, Bastarda, Fraktur, and Textura (shown here) were translated into some of the earliest European typefaces, and they remained in use in some countries well after the popularization of humanist letterforms.

Charlemagne revived political and social practices of the Roman Empire, including Roman lettering styles. His court letterers resurrected the forms of classical Roman capitals, using the letters' intellectual associations to give the Holy Roman Empire a mantle of legitimacy.

The major alphabetic legacy of this Carolingian period is its minuscule writing style. Distantly related to half-uncial scripts used by the Romans, the Carolingian minuscule developed as a standard book hand meant to replace the fragmented writing styles of western Europe. Carolingian minuscule is a clear, classical writing style whose steady rhythm is punctuated by straight and decisive ascenders and descenders. The minuscule would eventually evolve into the contemporary lowercase alphabet, and today's readers can easily read and recognize most of its shapes.

Although the minuscule did not immediately catch on throughout the continent, its impact was felt centuries later through the work of Renaissance writers and artists. Italian humanist scholars and letterers moved away from the prevailing gothic styles that had supplanted the Carolingian minuscule, turning once again to ancient Rome and its classical letterforms. Their new, humanist writing style synthesized minuscule and Romanesque gothic forms with the roundness, openness, and regularity of classical Roman lettering. These *lettera antica* reflect a renewed interest in classical Roman and Greek art, literature, and design. It was this style that Italian printers would translate into type later in the fifteenth century.

While the first European metal typefaces directly copied the pen-written structure of gothic letters, some Italian typographers were beginning to distill typographic letterforms from their handwritten cousins. Venetian printers such as Nicolas Jenson (c. 1420–1480) and Aldus Manutius (c. 1450–1515) designed and

500	600	700
LATE ROMAN & CHRISTIAN		INSULAR

UNCIALS
Formal book hands that synthesize elements of Roman capitals, cursives, and rustics.

CHRISTIAN STYLES
Looser compositions and lettering influenced by the Greek alphabet.

 **INSULAR, MEROVINGIAN STYLES**
New styles from the British Isles and France that are less rooted in Roman tradition.

HALF-UNCIALS
Alphabets with ascenders and descenders that use both cursive and uncial forms.

Ornate gothic capitals, c. 1524

Giovanni Antonio Tagliente

The decorative flourishes and geometric motifs of this Mannerist calligraphy are a prelude to the even more flamboyant lettering that European writing masters would create in the following century.

commissioned some of the early and most influential roman typefaces. Though informed by *lettera antica*, these typographers did not merely imitate existing writing. Instead, they regularized their letters into shapes that are more sculpted than handwritten. This transformation from writing to type reflected a classical and rationalist approach, but, as significantly, it emphasized the new tools and methods used to produce type. Carving and filing away the shapes of metal typefaces brought a new mechanization to letters that untethered type from the pen and set the stage for developments that followed.

Fifteenth-century Venice was a center of Renaissance trade and printing, and the widely admired designs of the Venetian printers' roman type spread throughout Europe. Looking beyond the handwritten form, European printers and typographers continued to rationalize the alphabet. From the sixteenth through the eighteenth century, type became progressively more structured and abstract. Type designers such as William Caslon, Pierre Simon Fournier, and John Baskerville created typefaces that moved farther away from the pen-written letter. Giambattista Bodoni, Firmin Didot, and others developed intensely rationalist typefaces that owe more to mechanical construction than to the fluidity of handwriting. These transitional and modern typefaces include few of early type's ligatures and alternate glyphs, which were meant to impersonate the motion and eccentricities of handwriting.

As typography became more rationalized, some letterers moved in the opposite direction. By the sixteenth century, type had eliminated much of the need for scribes and copyists. To distinguish their art from typography, master letterers created writing manuals that taught intricate forms of cursive handwriting to an expanding literate class. These writing and lettering styles exhibit Mannerist and

900	1000	1100
CAROLINGIAN / HOLY ROMAN EMPIRE		ROMANESQUE

 CAROLINGIAN MINUSCULE

A new alphabet partially based on half-uncial script—the origins of today's lowercase alphabet.

 **POST-CAROLINGIAN STYLES**

Forms influenced by, but starting to diverge from, Carolingian traditions.

CAROLINGIAN STYLES

Along with Carolingian minuscule, a general revival of classical Roman letter styles.

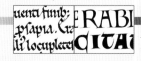 **ROMANESQUE**

New, experimental forms showing increased contrast—precursors to gothic styles.

Baroque tendencies—exaggerations in form and axis—and their scripts incorporate ornamental swashes and elaborate flourishes that cannot be mistaken for metal type. Fraktur, the gothic counterpart to Mannerist and Baroque styles, mixes angular pen-drawn forms with high-contrast, often extraneous embellishments. Created as both lettering and type, Fraktur's "broken letters" remained popular in the Germanic countries long after roman styles became the norm elsewhere in Europe.

As the Industrial Revolution of the eighteenth and nineteenth centuries accelerated Western society's commercial aspect, it dramatically affected the forms and uses of type and lettering. Signage for businesses and buildings took on a more prominent role, and the demand for novel letterforms increased. During this period, type designers began looking beyond traditional typography and classical writing to the less-restrained work of lettering artists and sign painters. Certain gothic styles were revived, and new, fanciful takes on decorative lettering found widespread use. Making use of technologies such as wood type, foundries and designers exaggerated and reinterpreted modern letters in outrageous and inventive ways, creating radically bold "fat faces," whose thick, ink-hungry strokes made them a prominent fixture on advertisements and other printed materials.

Fat faces and other imaginative new styles made the nineteenth century one of type design's most fertile periods and laid the groundwork for contemporary display lettering. Perhaps the most important development of this time was the sans serif letter. While classical and isolated instances of sans serif lettering exist throughout Western history (many Greek inscriptions lack obvious serifs) unserifed forms had not caught on among letterers or type designers. A neoclassical revival of Greek culture and architecture coincided with the insatiable desire for fresh styles

3. Nicolete Gray, *A History of Lettering* (Oxford: Phaidon Press, 1986), 173.

4. William Morris, "Art and Its Producers" (republished from the essay of the same title, 1901, by the William Morris Internet Archive, www.marxists.org/archive/morris).

1300	1400	1500
GOTHIC		RENAISSANCE

HUMANIST

A balanced writing style synthesizing Carolingian and Romanesque hands with classical Roman forms and proportions.

GOTHIC

Angular, compressed book hands that are often paired with ornate, rounded capitals.

RENAISSANCE TYPE

Movable type expressing Italian printers' classical and humanist design sensibilities.

ITALICS, MANNERISM

Script hands and type with more exaggerated forms and axes.

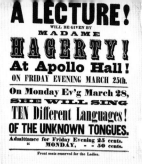

A Lecture!
Broadside, 1853
In place of classical typography's reserved palette of font styles, nineteenth-century printers combined many outlandish, unrelated fonts. This American poster mashes together novel styles such as slab serifs, fat faces, and decorative typefaces.
Library of Congress, Rare Book and Special Collections Division.

and likely played a role in the invention of nineteenth-century sans serif letters,[3] which began to appear in the work of sign painters and letterers. New media and applications such as router-cut wood type and sculptural signage were ideally suited to no-nonsense sans serif forms.

The unbridled commercialism and laissez-faire approach to nineteenth-century letters inevitably provoked a backlash. Artists of the Arts and Crafts, Art Nouveau, and similar movements returned in the late 1800s to the artisan production values of the early Renaissance and pre-printing era, emphasizing craft above commercialism. Calligraphers and typographers like Edward Johnston (1872–1944) and William Morris (1834–1896) dismissed the mass-produced, typically crude fat faces in favor of humanist, often hand-drawn letterforms. Many of these artists viewed their work in a communitarian light—William Morris saw handcraft as a tool to vanquish "the great intangible machine of commercial tyranny which oppresses the lives of all of us."[4] Such renewed faith in the handmade caused letterers to gravitate toward a more personal and organic alphabet, reviving both gothic and humanist traditions. An increasing number of artists, architects, and other

MODERN MOVEMENTS

POSTMODERNISM

Deconstructed type and digital experiments.

PSYCHEDELIA, POP REVIVALISM

Warped letterforms and a revival of nineteenth-century styles.

MODERNISM

Rationalized, precise forms, putting Bauhaus ideals into practice.

BAUHAUS

Geometric and mechanical forms.

DADA

Lettering and type that celebrate the chaotic and absurd.

DE STIJL

Elemental, geometric, and grid-based letters.

1700   **1800**
BAROQUE   NEOCLASSICAL   NINETEENTH-CENTURY

BAROQUE, ROCOCO

Letters in which the axis varies widely as type moves farther from its origins; increasingly embellished letters.

MODERN/NEOCLASSICAL

Rationalized letterforms with a vertical axis and increased stroke contrast.

FRAKTUR

A gothic blackletter style used mainly in northern European countries.

ARTS AND CRAFTS

A revival of handcrafted forms inspired by classical and medieval styles.

ART NOUVEAU

Organic, fluid, and expressive letterforms.

ADVERTISING TYPE

Bold, extreme, and experimental letters, often ornamental or geometric.

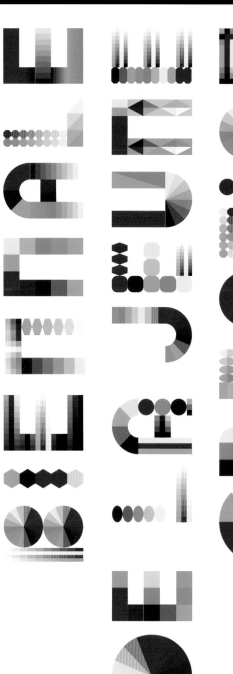

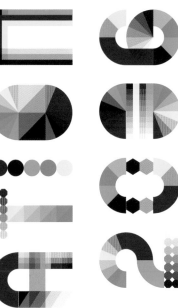

Biennale de la jeune création 2006

Arts plastiques, théâtre, musique, et danse

Houilles
24 mars - 7 avril

Exposition et spectacles
des jeunes créateurs

Artistes en résidence
Drôle de Sire
Ktha compagnie
La métonymie

Plateau rock
Mon Côté Punk
Romain Humeau
Hushpuppies
Stuck in the Sound

Renseignements
01 30 86 33 82
www.ville-houilles.fr

VILLE DE
HOUILLES

Avec le soutien de l'Adam 78,
du Conseil général des Yvelines et d'Arcadi

Graphisme : Fanette Mellier - Impression : Sérigraphie Moderne

UNKT der vergangenheit war
lle variationen des alten ›neu
ber es war nicht ›das‹ neue·
ürfen nicht vergessen′ dass

*Jan Tschichold's universal alphabet, designed in
1929, uses only straight lines and circles to build the
letters and phonetic marks of this single-case font.*

**Typographic Collage
from Les mots en liberté
futuristes**
Filippo Tommaso Marinetti,
1919

Opposite:
**Biennale de la Jeune
Creation**
Fannette Mellier, 2006
*Digital color calibration marks
become lettering on this art
exhibition poster.*

nontraditional letterers began to move letterforms into a more abstract realm beyond
the conventional shapes of the roman alphabet.

The mechanized brutality of World War I effectively ended the Art Nouveau
movement and ushered in several new strains of lettering and typographic experimentation. Dadaists and Futurists sought to destroy the meaning of language by
pushing the boundaries of legibility and readability. Modernist designers in the
de Stijl movement and at the Bauhaus experimented with scrupulously geometric
interpretations of the alphabet that removed all humanist traces from their letterforms. Melding the machine age with populist and socialist ideals, Bauhaus designers
attempted to create pure and mechanical forms of the alphabet, unencumbered by
history's baggage.

Like the refinements applied to the roman alphabet in the late Renaissance, the
technological advances and experimentation of the avant-garde found a more refined
and practical voice in the mid-twentieth century. Typefaces like Helvetica and Univers
embody a modernized, postwar society pushing toward a more utopian outlook. It
is not too much of a stretch to say that the same forces of order and affluence that
midwifed the Roman uppercase and Renaissance typography informed midcentury
modernist type design.

Through the twentieth century and to the present, cycles of experimentation
and codification have grown progressively shorter. Midcentury modernism was
rejected by the psychedelic styles of the 1960s. Psychedelia was in turn co-opted
as pop typography and was followed in quick succession by postmodernism and
digital typography. The compression of typographic history is reflected in contemporary lettering and type. The 1990s modernist revival, digital experimentation, and
a reinvigoration of handmade lettering have all taken place against the backdrop
of the internet, where the entire history of type and lettering rests at designers'
fingertips. Myriad styles live side by side in an exponentially growing volume of
online content, while words and letters play an even more central role in day-to-day
life. Simultaneously, the knowledge and tools for conceiving lettering and type have
become more accessible, spreading to a more diverse section of the population.
Although the power to define and dictate the standards of the alphabet is less concen-
trated, it is no less potent.

SYSTEMS &
TYPE-OLOGIES

SYSTEMS

Any lettering or type is based on a system. Like a moral code for the alphabet, typographic systems are sets of visual rules and guidelines that govern the actions and decisions involved in creating letters. These implicit systems enable characters to work together, by regulating and defining their appearance—dictating their shapes and sizes, how they fit together, and their visual spirit, as well as all other underlying tenets of the letters. Lacking a strong code, a lettering treatment or typeface rarely leads a successful life.

Analyzing and defining a typographic system is a bit like playing Twenty Questions. Instead of "Animal, vegetable, or mineral?" one might ask, "Serif, sans serif, or mixed?" Are the characters all the same width, or do they vary from letter to letter? If there are serifs, what shapes do they take? Are the round characters flat sided or curved? Do the letters lock together, or are the spaces between them irregular? The more questions one asks and answers, the better one can understand or create a typographic system. A well-established system constitutes the core of any typeface.

Either consciously or unconsciously, type designers build and follow rules that direct the myriad choices involved in creating a font. If a designer elects to draw letters with very round curves, this decision affects every curved character in the alphabet. If one or two letters do not reflect the system's curves, they appear uncomfortable and out of place within the font. Even relatively minor choices like the size of an i's dot are telegraphed throughout the character set. Each decision that affects an alphabet's visual code or the way that any letters relate to each other is part of the typographic system. By closely adhering to a system, a designer creates a typeface whose characters interact in a natural and consistent way.

Matchstick Alphabet (detail)
Alphabet, 2008
Lusine Sargsyan
Matchsticks radiate from letter skeletons formed by the bright red match tips, creating an almost three-dimensional effect. The unusual material unites (and potentially ignites) the eccentric characters of this flammable alphabet.

52

Above:
Miss Universum
Typeface, 2005
Hjärta Smärta

Right:
Neon letters
Alphabet, 2008 (ongoing)
Hjärta Smärta

Like a ransom note, each of these alphabets employs a palette of mismatched letters, building an unconventional typographic system based on the random and the unique qualities of each character. A shared physical material rather than the forms of the letters unifies the recycled neon sign alphabet.

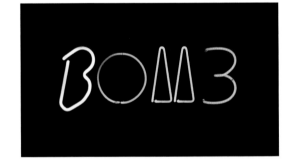

here, in my **Blazin'** jetliner **oen**

van

Composite
Typeface, 2002
Bruce Willen
Distinctively shaped counters, flat-sided characters, and selective use of slab serifs define the system of Composite. A typographic system is developed by applying these traits consistently throughout the alphabet.

Freight Text
Typeface, 2005
Joshua Darden

Freight's italic combines softly curved forms with angled, chiseled edges. Sharp, wedge serifs are juxtaposed with rounded, ball-shaped terminals, reinforcing the typeface's overall palette of round and faceted shapes.

Mg

BENDING THE RULES
Sometimes introducing counterintuitive elements into a typographic system yields unexpected results. While some other sans serifs from the turn of the twentieth century, such as Akzidenz Grotesk, include a more appropriate single-story version of the letter, Franklin Gothic's anomalous g and the font's slightly exaggerated stroke contrast give the typeface added warmth and individuality.

Typographic systems do not always remain static. Only the most rigid idea-driven systems of conceptual alphabets stay completely true to their origins. For the typical lettering treatment, alphabet, or font, the designer constantly refines and revisits the governing system as the project progresses. Sometimes a specific character presents new challenges to the system, forcing the designer to revise the parameters. New letters or words might suggest improved solutions to previously drawn forms. Creating lettering and type is a lengthy process involving numerous revisions to individual characters as well as to the typographic system.

As one-of-a-kind creations, lettering and handwriting accept more elastic relationships between the characters, but systems govern them much as they do typefaces. Unlike type, each lettered or written character is created for the specific instance or word in which it is used, allowing the designer greater leeway to define the system. Since the letters themselves do not have to adapt to multiple situations, their forms can be much more specific or unique. A lettering treatment may even contain many versions of a single character that are visually united through the style or personal hand of the letterer. Since the visual relationships between letters are the engine of any lettering system, a consistent visual framework drives lettering just as much as it does type—systems make letters work.

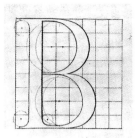
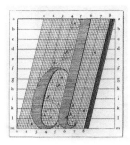

Romain du Roi
Engraved alphabet, 1692–1702
Louis Simonneau

Futura: Preliminary Drawings and Final Lowercase Type
Drawings, 1925. Typeface, 1927
Paul Renner
Like similar experiments by other modernist designers, the letters of Futura began with purely geometric circles and straight lines. The final typeface makes accommodations to legibility and typographic tradition, adapting its geometric concept to the world of functional typography. Futura's fine balance between the ideal and the practical has sustained the typeface's popularity since its debut.

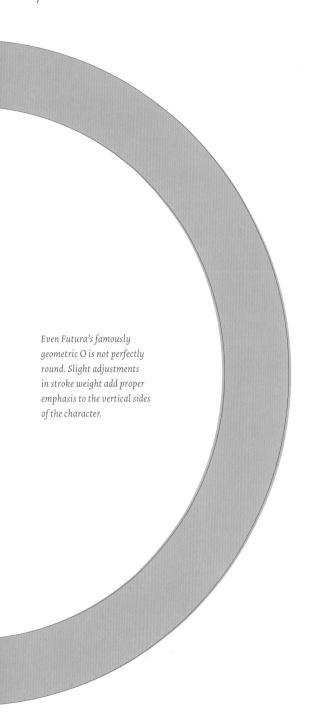

Even Futura's famously geometric O is not perfectly round. Slight adjustments in stroke weight add proper emphasis to the vertical sides of the character.

Although Futura is based on geometric ideals, concessions such as narrowing the width of letters and tapering strokes at connection points improve the font's legibility and overall functionality.

THE IDEAL VERSUS THE PRACTICAL

Attempts to rationalize and standardize the alphabet are a recurring theme throughout the history of lettering and typography. Countless artists, designers, scientists, and even governments have developed model letterforms that embody their philosophy or ideals of beauty and reflect the social and technological context of their eras.

Renaissance scholars and artists applied a newly analytical approach to science, art, and the alphabet, drafting complex geometric templates to construct idealized roman letters. As typography spread throughout Europe, these exercises further deemphasized the handwritten origin of the alphabet, a trend that continued through the following centuries.

In the 1690s at the behest of the French Académie des Sciences, a royal committee began studying letter design, with the goal of developing an official royal alphabet. More than a decade later, the committee presented the resulting *romain du roi* (king's roman) against a finely engraved grid (to which the letters did not always conform). Robert Bringhurst designates the *romain du roi* as the first neoclassical typeface, because of its strict vertical axis, and the alphabet's italic includes early examples of sloped roman forms.[1]

The *romain du roi* sought much of its inspiration in classical Roman letterforms—considered the pinnacle of letter design by many artists and typographers— and idealized Roman lettering continued to inspire constructed alphabets from a variety of sources. In the early twentieth century a new utopian model took hold, as modernist experimenters reduced the alphabet to basic geometries of circles and straight lines. Influenced by the logic and efficiency of modernism, designers such as Jan Tschichold (1902–1974) and the Bauhaus's Herbert Bayer (1900–1985) created highly rationalized geometric letterforms. These alphabets were far removed from the alphabet's handwritten origins, as they imagined the letter reduced to its purest mechanical forms.

Creating lettering or type is a tug-of-war between the ideal and the practical— the system's concept versus its functionality. The most successful typefaces and lettering treatments finely balance the aspirations and constrictions of their concept with the compromises, idiosyncrasies, and practicalities of application and legibility. Renaissance designers of utopian alphabets discovered the limitations of applying an inflexible and uniform system to a fundamentally subjective and irrregular subject. Likewise, the rigid geometries of the Bauhaus experiments found a more practical and applicable voice in modernist typefaces such as Futura, Helvetica, and Univers, which

1. Robert Bringhurst, *The Elements of Typographic Style*, version 2.5 (Point Roberts, WA: Hartley and Marks, 2002), 129.

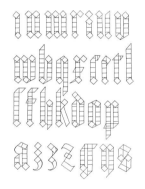

Underweysung Der Messung

Constructed alphabet, 1525 Albrecht Dürer

German artist Dürer wrote several treatises that mathematically analyze subjects as diverse as the human form, perspective drawing, and the alphabet. While Dürer managed to rationalize many of the characters in this gothic alphabet, when he was confronted with less regular forms, the idiosyncrasies of handwriting crept into his formula.

Optic
SCANR
01234
56789

Perhaps an ultimate expression of mechanically inspired type, the forms of OCR and MICR fonts (optical character recognition and magnetic ink character recognition) were first developed in the 1950s and 1960s specifically to be read by digital scanners.

Opposite:
Having Guts
Lettering installations, 2003
Stefan Sagmeister with
Matthias Ernstberger, Miao
Wang, and Bela Borsodi
The words in this series of constructed lettering treatments appear and vanish as the camera angle, lighting, or arrangement of objects changes.
Photos by Bela Borsodi.

Fire in the Hole
Alphabet, 2006
Oliver Munday
Burned and disfigured toy soldiers summon a host of outside associations to this alphabet.

successfully infuse the hand-derived forms of the roman alphabet with rationalized qualities. Most type designers and letterers take this pragmatic approach, balancing their ideal system with the requirements of legibility, utility, and context.

CONCEPTUAL ALPHABETS AND LETTERING

While the majority of fonts and lettering treatments accept the practicalities of legibility, some designers refuse to compromise their original vision and system. These conceptual letters or alphabets rarely aim to create the most readable text, and their letterforms occasionally lack recognizably alphabetic characteristics. Instead, conceptual alphabets illustrate or embody ideas, sets of constraints, and editorial perspectives, illustrating their concepts through letterforms rather than strictly pictorial means.

All type and lettering treatments begin with a concept, whether straightforward or elaborate. What sets conceptual letters apart is a rigid adherence to their guiding principles above other concerns. Sometimes these alphabets tackle complex subjects or associations, typographically translating an abstract idea, opinion, or process. Other conceptual letters, such as the geometrically constructed alphabets of the Renaissance, apply a rigid formula to their structure, forcing their forms into the constraints of an inflexible system. Like performance art, many conceptual alphabets emphasize their creation process, with the end result being less important than how they get there. A process-oriented alphabet may force its designer to create letterforms under a very specific set of conditions or with a particular, sometimes unusual, set of tools.

Unlike typical fonts or letters, some conceptual alphabets do not strive to convey a particular lettering style or look, and the result may surprise even the alphabet's creator. Conceptual letters can take the form of a lettering treatment, word, or poster created for a particular application. Others exist only in A–Z form and are never arranged into words. An increasing number of contemporary artists and designers view the alphabet as a subject for art and experimentation, not just a set of tools used to convey language. Conceptual letters are dedicated to their idea above all else.

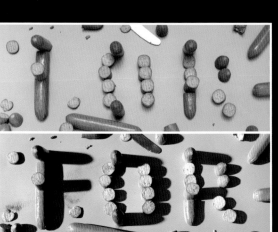

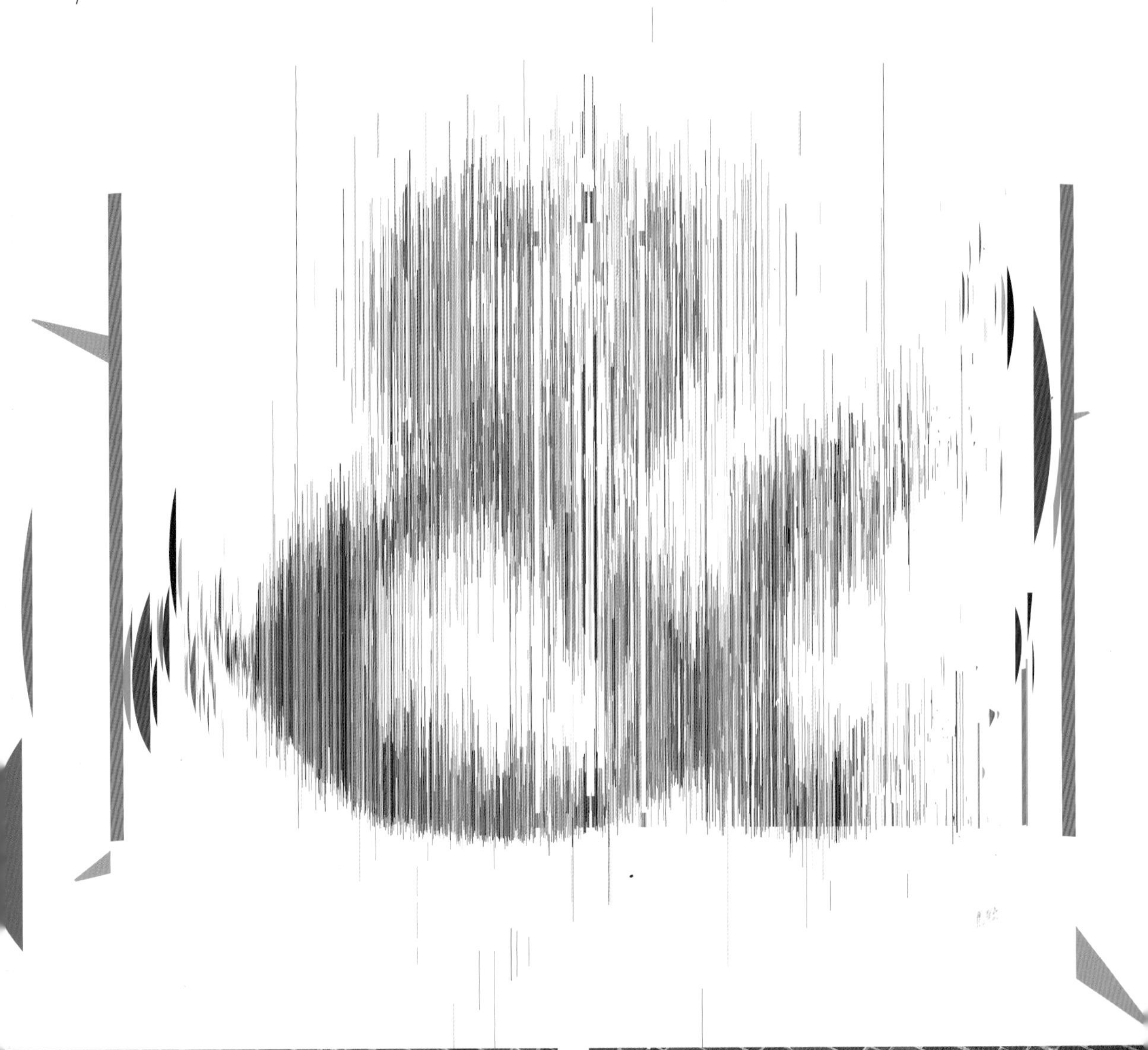

Years of love have
been forgotten in the
hatred of a
minute

Opposite:

Slitscan Type Generator
Adobe Illustrator script, 2006
Jonathan Keller
A custom computer script automatically generates this alphabet by slicing and recombining the letters of every font on a user's computer. The script produces different results depending on the quantity and styles of fonts that a particular user has installed.

Right:

Imageability: Paths, Edges, Nodes, Districts, Landmarks
Font family, 2002
Michael Stout
Based on Kevin Lynch's classic urban planning book, Image of the City, this series of fonts charts the forms of the alphabet through Lynch's five identifiers for mapping and navigating the urban environment.

Far right:

Conjoined Font
Typeface, 2006
Post Typography
Each character in this typeface connects to others on a square grid, turning text into a semi-abstract typographic pattern.

Below:

Years of Love
Lettering installation, 2008
Hayley Griffin
Using birdseed as her medium, the designer executed several lettering treatments in a Baltimore park and photographed them over three days.

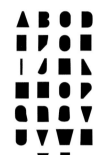

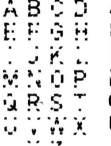

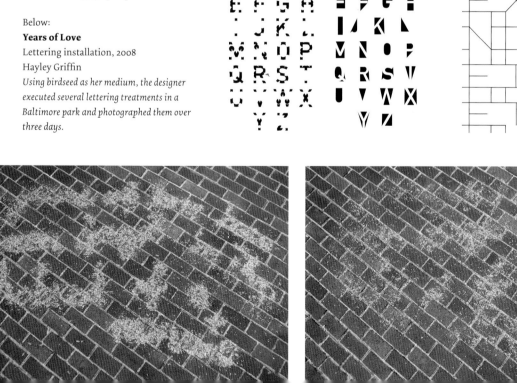

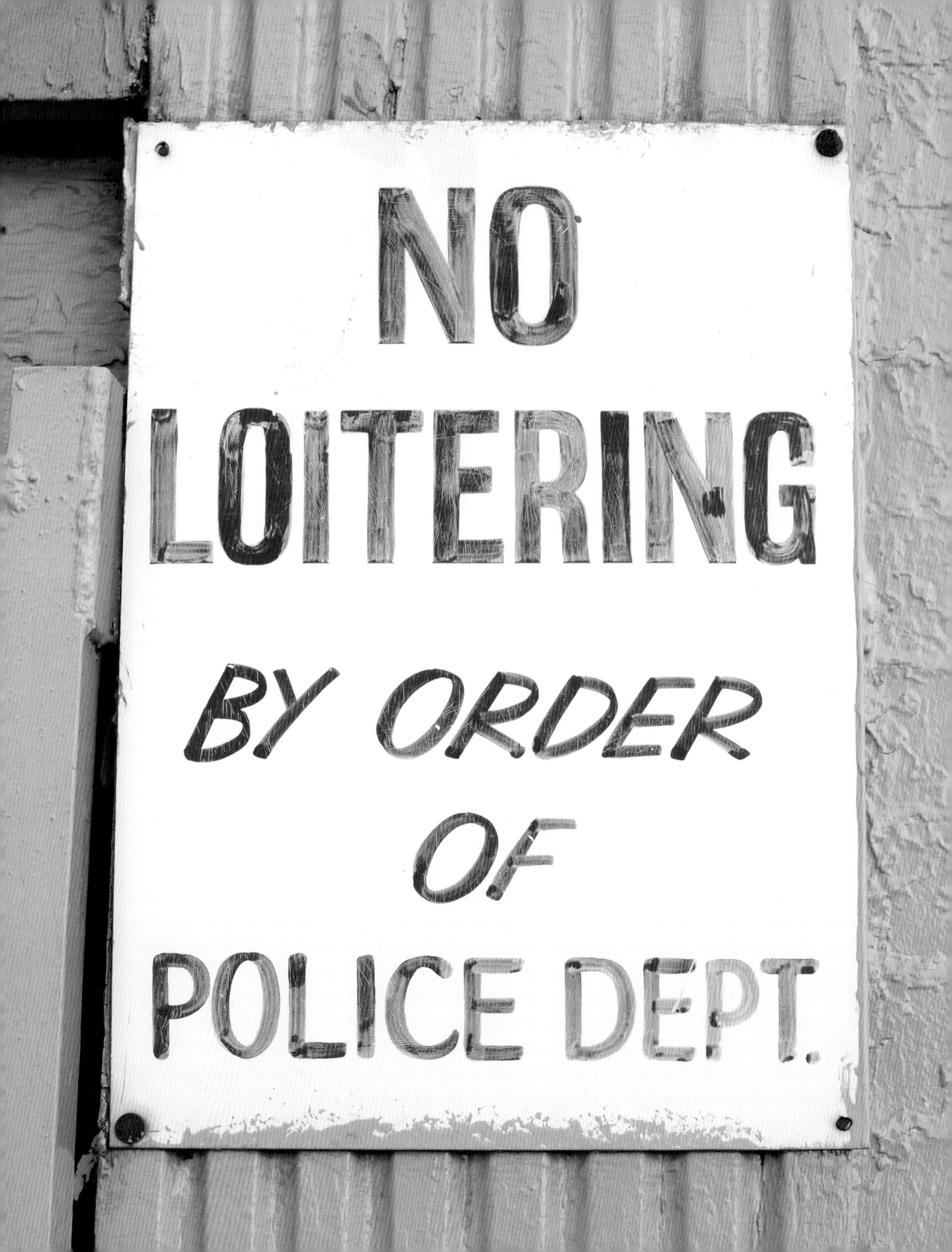
NO
LOITERING
BY ORDER
OF
POLICE DEPT.

WRITING, LETTERING, OR TYPE?

Writing, lettering, and type represent three distinct methods of creating letters. A written letter or word is created with very few strokes of the writing implement—think of cursive handwriting or a hastily scrawled note. Lettering builds the form of each character from multiple, often numerous, strokes or actions—a love note meticulously carved into a tree trunk or a hand-drawn letterform in graffiti, for instance. Type is a palette of ready-made shapes, enabling the reproduction of similar- or identical-looking letters through a single action—like summoning digital characters from a keyboard or pressing a rubber stamp on a sheet of paper.

Writing emphasizes quick communication and execution above appearance. Until the development of typography and, crucially, the spread of digital correspondence, handwriting's relative speed and ease made it the most reasonable method for written communication. Imagine how long it would take to carefully draw each letter of a grocery list, and the advantages of a legible and efficient writing system become clear. This is not to suggest that writing is unconcerned with the aesthetics of letters. On the contrary, many handwriting methods and primers throughout the centuries have espoused the handwriting styles that their authors considered most beautiful or legible. The ability to write well, in terms of aesthetics as well as articulateness, was regarded as an integral part of literacy and education.

Lettered characters are constructed through multiple actions and may involve several tools or processes. A digitally drawn logo, a neon sign, and a chiseled inscription on a church doorway are all examples of lettering. Like writing, lettering is a one-of-a-kind creation, designed for a specific application. Even master letterers cannot duplicate exactly the same form from one instance to another—variations inevitably occur. Lettering differs from handwriting in that its main focus is usually on technique and visual appearance. While speed may be important, it is generally less so than the end product. More than it does in writing and type, context influences the way lettering looks. The uniqueness of each lettering treatment allows its designer flexibility and creativity to respond to a given context in very specific ways. Letters can be compressed, warped, or interlocked to fit a particular space. Words can be built from the most appropriate medium or material, from pencil to stainless steel to chocolate syrup.

This faded, hand-lettered sign reveals the multiple brushstrokes used to build each character. Although it lacks the defining characteristics of type, careful lettering can mimic typography.

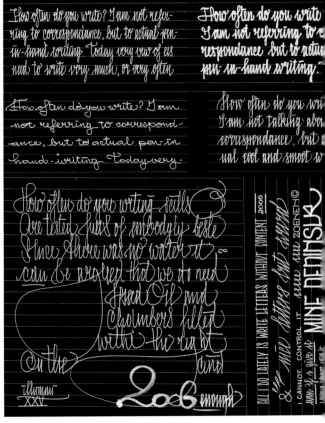

Sketchbook pages

Calligraphy, 2006–2007

Letman (Job Wouters)

Some calligraphy blurs the line between handwriting and lettering. As letterforms grow more polished and embellished, they become more lettering-like. In some cases the artist's intent may be the only distinction between an expertly written paragraph and a quickly lettered word.

No War

Monumental lettering, 2003

Verena Gerlach

Designed to protest the war in Iraq, this lettering installation uses a matrix of lit windows to form letters. The words become legible as building occupants leave for the evening and switch off (or leave on) the lights in each room.

Hey There

Hey There

WRITING

Hey There

Hey There

LETTERING

Hey There

Hey There

TYPE

Quick cursive and print hands are two common forms of writing. As characters become more painstakingly executed or constructed, they become lettering. Type occasionally mimics writing or lettering styles with its ready-made palette of shapes.

Los Feliz
Typeface, 2002
Christian Schwartz with
Zuzana Licko and Rudy
VanderLans, Emigre.
Original sign lettering by
Cosmo Avila
Los Feliz is based on hand-lettered signs on an auto parts store in Los Angeles. The final typeface retains many of the idiosyncrasies of the original lettering, but standardizes them into a more regular system.
Photos by Matthew Tragesser.

Lettered or written characters that can be reproduced and rearranged become type. Type unites the detail and formality of lettering with the speed and ease of handwriting. The ability to create and reproduce preexisting characters through a single action differentiates type from writing and lettering. Reproduction methods have varied and evolved over the centuries. Metal and wood typefaces, rub-down transfer letters, typewriters, rubber stamps, stencils, photo lettering, and digital fonts are all examples of type. Type's strength and beauty lie in its ability to look the same in any context. One can type an A thousands of times and achieve a consistent result, yet writing or lettering the same character will produce variations. Type also constitutes a system of powerful relationships, which transform a palette of shapes into a true kit of parts capable of endless recombinations. Like any set of tools, type has power that is measured not just by individual elements but also by how the parts work together. Unlike lettered and written characters, each typographic glyph must be ready to redeploy into a new word formation at any time.

Thanks to digital technologies, typography has usurped many of writing's long-held roles. It is much faster and more practical to write letters, take notes, or chart finances by typing on a computer than by handwriting these communications. Likewise, graphic designers have replaced lettering artists with digital fonts that can quickly reproduce effects similar, though not usually equal, to custom lettering. The loss of personality and individuality found in handwriting and lettering is an unfortunate side effect of the proliferation of type. Nonetheless, an exponentially growing library of new and more sophisticated typefaces keeps increasing the range of type's voice.

LOS FELIZ
Power Steering Pumps
Specialist
Fuel Injector Computer
Steering Gears
DETAILING

LETTER STRUCTURE

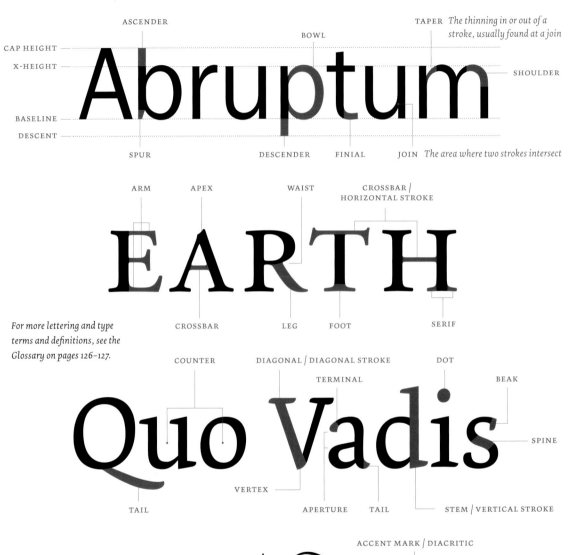

ASCENDER

BOWL

TAPER *The thinning in or out of a stroke, usually found at a join*

CAP HEIGHT

X-HEIGHT

SHOULDER

Abruptum

BASELINE

DESCENT

SPUR

DESCENDER

FINIAL

JOIN *The area where two strokes intersect*

ARM

APEX

WAIST

CROSSBAR / HORIZONTAL STROKE

EARTH

For more lettering and type terms and definitions, see the Glossary on pages 126–127.

CROSSBAR

LEG

FOOT

SERIF

COUNTER

DIAGONAL / DIAGONAL STROKE

DOT

TERMINAL

BEAK

Quo Vadis

SPINE

TAIL

VERTEX

APERTURE

TAIL

STEM / VERTICAL STROKE

ACCENT MARK / DIACRITIC

EYE

SWASH

M. Crüe

FINIAL

STROKE *A single mark and motion of the writing implement; when applied to type or built-up lettering, the term is more figurative*

PUNCTUATION

CONNECTING STROKE

BRACKETED / ADNATE SERIF

UNBRACKETED / ABRUPT SERIF

REFLEXIVE *A serif that implies an abrupt change in the direction of the stroke, such as that found at the feet of most roman letters*

TRANSITIVE *A serif that suggests a continuous motion into or out of a stroke, such as on most italics*

BILATERAL SERIF

UNILATERAL SERIF

CALLIGRAPHIC SERIF, ASYMMETRICAL

CUPPED SERIF

WEDGE SERIF

BRACKETED SERIF

UNBRACKETED SERIF

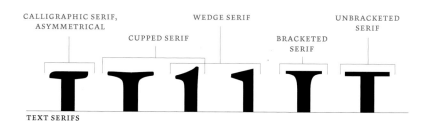

TEXT SERIFS

SLAB SERIF

CLARENDON (BRACKETED SLAB)

LATIN

TUSCAN

ANTIQUE TUSCAN

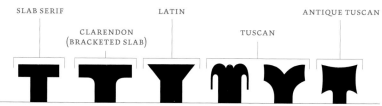

DISPLAY SERIFS AND NINETEENTH-CENTURY STYLES

SERIFS AND TERMINALS *represent the entrance and exit marks of the pen. The origins of various serif shapes relate to different writing styles, tools, pen angles, and amounts of pressure. By the eighteenth and nineteenth centuries, the forms of serifs and terminals had become detached from their calligraphic origins, as type designers and sign painters treated serifs as separate ornamental or geometric elements.*

TEARDROP TERMINAL

BALL TERMINAL, BRACKETED

BALL TERMINAL, UNBRACKETED

SHEARED TERMINAL

BEAK

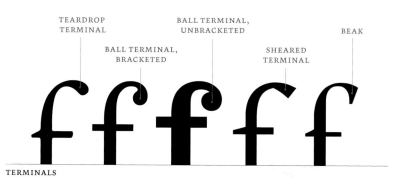

TERMINALS

AXIS *refers to the angle of emphasis within a letter or stroke. Letters or typefaces with modulated strokes have areas of thicks and thins, visible in rounded characters like the o or a. Typefaces derived from broad-nibbed pen writing typically have a diagonal axis that reflects the angle of the pen's tip. Multiple axes can exist within the same font or letter. Axis differs from slope, which refers to the angle or slant of an italic or oblique font.*

(See also Angle of Translation on page 52.)

CONTRAST *is the amount of variation from thick to thin within and between the strokes of a character. Without any contrast or stroke modulation, letters suffer from uneven color, and their horizontal strokes appear optically thicker than their stems.*

The X-HEIGHT *is the vertical measurement of a lowercase letter's main body, usually defined by the x. It differs from typeface to typeface. Increasing a font's x-height increases the apparent size of the letters and generally improves legibility at small sizes. An excessively large x-height can have the opposite effect, reducing the overall readability of word shapes and making the letters seem graceless. An x-height that is too small can produce letters that look top-heavy or stunted.*

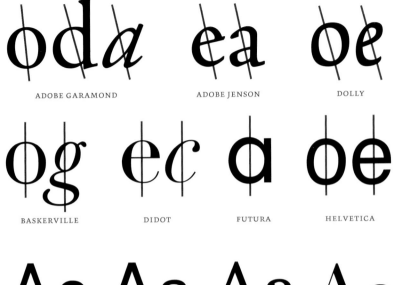

ADOBE GARAMOND

ADOBE JENSON

DOLLY

BASKERVILLE

DIDOT

FUTURA

HELVETICA

Aa
Letters drawn with no stroke contrast
Aa

Aa
SCALA SANS
low contrast
Aa

Aa
SCALA
medium contrast
Aa

Aa
DIDOT
high contrast
Aa

Rounded characters and pointed serifs extend slightly above the cap height or x-height and dip just below the baseline. These subtle overshoots optically compensate for the softness or pointedness of the forms—without an overshoot these characters would appear smaller than the flat or squared letters.

Ascenders may be taller than the cap height.

The x-height is generally greater than half of the cap height.

Exodus

Frost Celtic

Cochin has a small x-height.

Interstate has a large x-height.

TYPE AND LETTERING CLASSIFICATION

Like scientific classification, the categorization of letters and type enables one to better analyze and understand their traits, forms, and history. Printers and type historians first devised classification systems in the nineteenth century, providing order and categorization to an exploding menu of new type styles. The categories generally correspond to periods of art and intellectual history, from the humanist faces first used during the Renaissance to the transitional fonts of the neoclassical period. Different type foundries and scholars gave their own labels to letter classes, and the specific names and descriptions continue to generate disagreement today. Sans serif letters alone have been referred to as grotesks, grotesques, gothics, dorics, antiques, and lineals. The actual terms of classification, however, are less important than the characteristics and systems that they represent. One does not have to know the scientific term for a dog to know that it barks.

At their most useful, categories of lettering and type represent sets of attributes shared by many typefaces and lettering treatments. These classes give designers and typographers a solid starting point for discussing and analyzing typographic systems. Type categories are guideposts only, since their borders are not absolute. While most letter examples can fit into a single category, many defy neat classification. Just because the attributes of scripts and slab serifs seem incompatible does not mean that slab serif script letters do not exist. Some transitional or geometric sans serifs exhibit humanist influences, while semi serif or mixed serif fonts live with one foot in the serif and the other in the sans serif world. As experimentation continues, letterers and type designers are not constrained by the boundaries of traditional type categories.

Adobe Garamond

Humanist / Old Style

Renaissance- and Baroque-era type designers looked to Roman lettering and calligraphy as inspiration for their typefaces. These humanist letterforms incorporate elements of calligraphic handwriting such as the diagonal axis of the broad-nibbed pen and the softened, wedge serifs that replicate the pen stroke's starting point. Type designers continue to create contemporary revivals and interpretations of humanist forms.

Baskerville

Transitional / Neoclassical

Transitional serif letters retain humanist traces, yet their forms are more ordered and rationalized than old style characters. These rationalized features usually include a vertical axis, increased stroke contrast, and details that appear formalized and constructed, like symmetrical serifs.

Didot

Modern / Didone

Typefaces like Bodoni and Didot modernize and streamline the forms of the alphabet, pushing them farther from their humanist origins. Modern letters have a strictly vertical axis, heightened or extreme stroke contrast, and serifs that feel mechanically drawn or constructed rather than smoothly written.

Serifa

Slab Serif / Egyptian

As their name implies, slab serif letters possess squared-off serifs that abruptly extend from the character's main strokes. First developed in the early nineteenth century for signage and advertising printing, the slab serif, with its relatively uniform stroke weight, was a counterpart to the extreme stroke contrast of the popular Ultra Bodoni styles.

Clarendon

Clarendon

Clarendons are a specific subset of slab serif letters. Where the typical Egyptian's serifs terminate in angled, abrupt connections, a clarendon's serifs are bracketed (adnate) so that the serifs flow smoothly into the stem of the letterform. Many clarendons bear similarities to transitional and modern forms, exhibiting greater stroke variation than typical slab serifs.

Scala Sans

Humanist Sans Serif

Though sans serif type and lettering did not become popular until the twentieth century, examples of sans serif lettering exist in some Renaissance inscriptions and have precedent in classical Greek letterforms. The modulated stroke weight, greater contrast, and true italic versions of humanist sans serif letters convey a calligraphic influence, which in some cases even includes flared terminals that suggest serifs.

ITC Franklin Gothic

Transitional Sans Serif / Industrial or Realist Sans Serif

Transitional sans serif fonts, like their nineteenth-century counterpart, the slab serif, were developed as advertising display type, based on the work of contemporary sign painters. While the letter shapes are similar to serif forms, most of the handwritten qualities are missing, giving transitional sans serifs a more detached, functional quality. Typically, transitional sans serifs lack a true italic, display low stroke contrast, and appear rationalized and constructed.

Geometric Sans Serif

Based on geometric rather than humanist forms, the characters of geometric sans serifs are constructed around a basic set of elements—typically circles, triangles, and straight lines. This rigid design approach frequently imparts a modular and mathematical spirit to the letterforms. Although these alphabets were first developed in the early twentieth century, the proportions of some geometric sans serif letters bear a resemblance to those of classical Roman capitals.

Half Block / Octagonal

Another style popularized by nineteenth-century sign painters and wood type makers, half blocks are formed around an octagonal shape, using straight lines. While the angularity of their facets gives half blocks a geometric or machined quality, the use of straight lines to suggest complex curves can lend an unexpected subtlety to some letterforms.

Script / Cursive

Scripts include many lettering styles, from calligraphic to brush lettering to even mechanical and geometric letterforms. More than other type or lettering styles, scripts and cursives directly reference the handwritten origin of the alphabet. As in cursive handwriting, a connecting stroke often joins adjacent forms, creating words that flow from letter to letter. Reflecting the handwriting process, scripts generally employ italic rather than roman letterforms.

Decorative / Display / Ornamental

Decorative or display letters include any type or lettering with embellished or decorative forms. While they often exhibit attributes of other classes, display letters are specifically meant to be used at large sizes where their detailed or unconventional features work best. Since custom lettering is better suited than type to creating detailed, ornamental, or monumental letterforms, contemporary lettering often falls into this broad category.

Organic

Organic letterforms generally convey a human-made or natural origin. Their forms usually feel spontaneous, loose, or even grown, rather than built up and mechanically constructed. While many organic typefaces or letters can also be considered decorative, some fonts are surprisingly readable at text sizes and have a warm, handwritten feel.

Blackletter / Old English / Gothic

Gothic lettering styles were widely used throughout medieval Europe, and Johannes Gutenberg employed a gothic Textura as the first European printing type. Gothic letterforms unrepentantly display the strokes of the broad-nibbed pen, and the capitals are frequently ornamental and finely detailed. Poor legibility and strong associations confine most contemporary gothics to the realm of display lettering and type.

EXERCISE: FICTIONAL CHARACTERS

Type designers and letterers develop and follow typographic systems that guide the shapes of their letters. These underlying systems provide a structure for stringing together the inconsistent forms of the alphabet. A typographic system is also a formula for addressing new or unexpected shapes and situations.

Imagine that the fictional characters on this page are recent additions to the roman alphabet. How might a designer convincingly adapt these characters to an existing typeface with a well-defined system? Choosing several existing fonts (such as Franklin Gothic, Sabon, and Bodoni), closely analyze their traits and underlying system. Using their existing letterforms as a guide, draw each fictional character as if it were a member of the character set in the fonts that you have chosen. Whether a designer is constructing an a or a ʌ, typographic systems provide guideposts for creating letterforms.

abcdefꝉꝇllmɯ
opɹrstuvwxyz

Look at related shapes and letters as a guide for designing new forms. Where do the stroke emphasis and axis occur? How round are the curves? Which direction do serifs face? How tall are the ascenders and descenders?

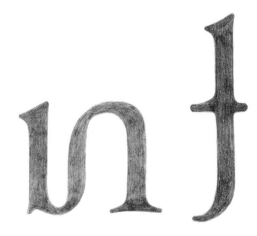

LETTERING BY SARA FRANTZMAN, BASED ON ADOBE GARAMOND

Exercise based on a tutorial by Jonathan Hoefler originally posted on www.typophile.com.

Some alphabet letters come in multiple flavors. The two-story and single-story versions of the lowercase a and g are used interchangeably, and some lettering treatments or fonts employ less-common cursive versions of letters like S and Q. Specific typographic systems, constraints, or styles dictate which version of a letterform is most appropriate. Script and italic alphabets frequently differ greatly from their roman counterparts; most true italics employ a single-story a, and many use a single-story g.

ag

ADOBE
GARAMOND

ag

FRANKLIN
GOTHIC

ag

UNITED

ag

FUTURA

Even the dot of an i can speak volumes for a typographic system. Dots may be circular, square, lopsided, calligraphic, or an unusual shape. The height of the dot above the stem and how it corresponds to the dots of punctuation marks affect the overall characteristics of a system.

ıíĩíi iii ıiı

Dolly
Drawings for typeface, 2001
Underware
While the evolution of type design has progressed from handwriting-derived forms toward ever more structural letter styles, some contemporary designers, especially in the Netherlands, have returned to the calligraphic origins of typography. Dolly (used to set the text of this book) is unabashedly based on pen-written lettering, giving it warmth and approachability.

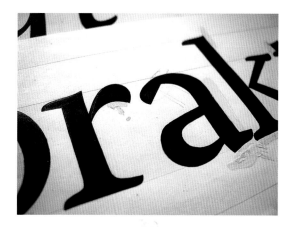

Before the development of photolithographic printing and digital typography, type was a three-dimensional object. To compose the text of books and periodicals, typographers placed each piece of metal or wood type by hand (or later by using a linecasting machine such as a Linotype). The flat area of a piece of type that makes contact with the paper is the type's face.

BOOK TYPEFACES

Book typefaces are the foundation of all typography. That the term *book* describes an entire genre of type, lettering, and handwriting is no accident. Fifteenth-century European printers first developed type based on formal writing styles used to reproduce manuscripts and books. These early typefaces translated the book hands of scribes into cast metal, creating new forms that did not merely imitate handwriting but also reinterpreted and regularized it. As this new technology replaced labor-intensive hand copying, typography sparked and enabled the almost universal literacy now taken for granted in many parts of the world. Despite the thousands of new and experimental font styles designed over the last two hundred years, serif book typefaces are the most read classes of letterforms, comprising the body type of most books and periodicals and many websites.

As the name implies, book typefaces are meant for setting large quantities of text at a single point size. Primary concerns for designers of book type are legibility and readability—the visual distinctions between each character and how well the letters convey their messages over the course of sentences and volumes. Since book type is typically used to set lengthy texts, the readability and visual flow of long passages is as important as the legibility of single words. Legibility studies have shown that the shapes and outlines of words are as important for comprehension as the forms of the letters themselves.[2] Individual capital letters may be more legible than lowercase, but uppercase sentences or paragraphs become more difficult to read without the distinctive up-and-down rhythm of the lowercase alphabet. The lowercase design is the most crucial element of a book typeface.

While serif fonts account for the bulk of book typefaces, many sans serif faces also work well as body copy. A well-made sans serif book face is no less legible than a serif font, although some readers have indicated a preference for serif type in long texts.[3] Sans serif book typefaces contain many nuances that facilitate their functionality at small point sizes. Book sans serifs typically have looser letterspacing than their all-purpose siblings, as well as increased tapering where two strokes meet. Some sans serif faces even add calligraphic forms to increase letter differentiation.

Style Wars

FUTURA

Style Wars

FUTURA BOOK

Some font families include a specific book style that differs from its roman font and is meant for setting small text.

2. Rolf F. Rehe, "Legibility," in *Graphic Design and Reading: Explorations of an Uneasy Relationship*, ed. Gunnar Swanson (New York: Allworth Press, 2000).

3. Ibid.

cælo delectatur hūecto. Iugero q̄ttuor modios uel tres ſpſiſſe ſufficiat.

⸿DE Siſamo ſerendo.   T.vii.

Vnc ſiſamum ſeritur putri ſolo uel pinguibus arenis uel terra cō
geſtitia. Iugero quattuor uel ſex ſeſtarios ſeuiſſe conueniet. Hoc
mēſe poſtremo·pria uice agros ſſcidemus:q̄ hituri ſūt medicam.

⸿DE Vicia fœnogræco & farragine ſerendis.   T.viii.

Vnc uiciæ prima ſatio eſt: et fœnigræci cum pabuli cauſa ſerunt.
Viciæ.vii.modii iugerum æque & fœnigræci ſemen implebit. Far
rago etiam loco reſtibili ſtercorato ſeritur. Hordei canterini ī iugero.x.
modios ſparginus circa æquinoctium: ut āte hyemē cōualeſcat. Si de
paſci.æpius uelis:uſq̄ ī maiū mēſe eius paſtura ſufficiet. Quod ſi ex ea
ſemē etiā reddigere:uſq̄ ad martias kaledas:& dehīc pecora ſphibebis.

⸿DE Lupino ſerendo.   T.ix.

Oc menſe:ut loca fœcundentur exilia:lupinus circa idus ſeratur.
Et ubi creuerit:uertente uomere putrefiat exciſus.

⸿DE Pratis nouellis formandis uel ueteribus excolendis.   T.x.

Vnc prata ſi libuerit:poſſumus nouella formare. Si eligendi fa
cultas eſt:locum pinguem roſidum planum leniter inclinatum:
uel huiuſmōi ualle deputabimus: ubi hūor nec ſtatī præcipitari cogit:
nec diu debet hærere. Poteſt quidē & ſoluto & gracili ſolo prati forma:
ſi rigetur:imponi. Extirpandus eſt itaq̄ locus hoc tempore: & liberan
dus impedimentis omnibus:uel herbis altioribus & ſolidis atq̄ uirgul
tis. Deinde cum frequēter exercitatus fuerit ac multa aratione ſolutus:
ſubmotis lapidibus & glebis ubiq̄ confractis ſtercoretur luna creſcente
recenti lætamine. Ab ungulis iumentorum ſumma intentione ſeruet
intactus:præcipue quotiens humeſcit:ne inæquale ſolum reddāt multis
locis impreſſa ueſtigia. Sed ſi prata uetera muſcus obduxerit: abraden
dus eſt:& ſcalptis eiſdem locis fœni ſpgenda ſunt ſemina : & quod ad
necandum muſcum prodeſt:cinis ſæpius ingerendus. Quod ſi ſterilis
factus eſt locus carie incuriæ uetuſtate exaret:ac de nouo rurſus æquet.
Nam prata ſterilia plerunq̄ arare conueniet. Sed in nouo prato rapa
conſerere poſſumus:quorū meſſe finita cætera quæ dicta ſunt: exeque
mur. Viciam tamen fœni ſeminibus mixtam poſt hoc ſpargemus. Ri
gari uero anteq̄ durū ſolū fecerit:nō debebit:ne eius cratē minus ſolidā
uis īterflui corrūpat humoris.   ⸿DE Vindemia celebrāda.   T.xi.

Oc menſe locis tepidis maritimiſq̄ celebranda uindemia eſt:frigi
dis apparanda. In doliis picādis hic modus erit:ut doliū ducetoȝ
congiorum.xii.libris picetur.deinde pro minoris extimatiōe ſubducas.
Sed maturitatem uindemiæ cognoſcimus hoc genere. Si expreſſa uua
uinacia quæ in acinis celant: hoc ē grana: fuſca & nonnulla ſppemodū

Opposite top:

Arnhem

Typeface, 1998–2002
Fred Smeijers, OurType
*Some recent type designers
have designed darker book
faces that recapture the
robustness of letterpress
printing. Arnhem, originally
created for a Dutch
newspaper, combines sharp
detailing with a solid stroke
weight and compact width.*

Page from De Re Rustica

Printed roman type, 1472
Nicholas Jenson
*Early printed books mixed type
with hand-lettered initials,
ornaments, and punctuation.*
Special Collections, University of
Iowa Libraries, Iowa City, Iowa.

...rst. And it is true that there are many good typefac...
...rs. But there are also many good typefaces made by p...
...ings, with some type designing on the side. By 'type'...
...sed within typography, so I refer to the fonts which a...
...ves out the area of handwriting, calligraphy, and lett...

Scala *Italic*

While serif fonts account for the bulk of book typefaces, many sans serif faces also work well as body copy.

Scala *Italic*

While serif fonts account for the bulk of book typefaces, many sans serif faces also work well as body copy.

Scala and Scala Sans
Type family, 1990–1993
Martin Majoor, FontFont
The serif and sans serif versions of Scala both work well as text typefaces. Calligraphic and humanist elements give Scala Sans a classical countenance while softening its forms.

4. Beatrice Warde, "The Crystal Goblet or Printing Should Be Invisible," in *Looking Closer 3: Classic Writings on Graphic Design*, edited by Michael Bierut, Jessica Helfand, Steven Heller, and Rick Poynor (New York: Allworth Press, 1999).

(such as a serifed capital I), more pronounced stroke contrast, and true italics. These distinctions improve the reproduction and legibility of small-scale sans serif type.

Small sizes are where book letters do most of their work. Typographers typically use book typefaces at sizes between six and twelve points. (This text is set at nine points.) As letters get smaller or more distant, fine details blur and disappear. Hairline serifs dissolve, and small openings close. Subtle modulation becomes lost among letters of uniform stroke weight. This is especially true at minute printing sizes, as viscous ink flows outward and expands into the paper. Most book type avoids extremely delicate detailing, or it harnesses the degradation process purposefully. Some fonts incorporate expanded counters and apertures to retain legibility; others possess sharp serifs, meant to round and retreat at small sizes; and some allow the printing process to soften their angular forms. Book faces often employ more generous widths and letterspacing to enhance legibility and readability.

A reader comparing book typefaces will notice that they all have a relatively similar range of typographic weight and color. Certain weights of text are easier to read than others—a novel printed entirely in an extra bold or lightweight font would drive away readers by the dozen. If one squints at a page of text, the paragraphs appear as gray blocks. Bolder fonts create a dark gray, while lighter fonts look paler. Some designers and typographers prefer light, airy pages while others favor denser, more solid text. Many early printed books featured dark pages of muscular letterforms that emulated the layout and spacing of handwritten manuscripts. As production techniques improved, it became possible to design type that retained fine detail through repeated inking and printing, allowing for lighter, sharper letters and pages.

Whether their book type is delicate or sturdy, most designers adhere to the idea that text typefaces are reserved containers for conveying written language. Design historian Beatrice Warde famously compared good typography to a clear crystal goblet, an unobtrusive vessel that allows one to appreciate and focus on the design's content.[4] While convincing arguments may be made against this maxim, especially about display lettering, book type's primary goal is still to effectively serve and present its content.

Bald Is Beautiful
T-shirt graphic, 2007
Nolen Strals

Many instances of successful display lettering are created for a one-time, site-specific use. Unlike type, which must function in multiple combinations and environments, display letters can adopt very individualized forms and arrangements to best suit their setting.

DISPLAY LETTERING AND TYPE

More so than small-scale book type, display lettering expresses the tone and spirit of a design. Although book styles can function at display sizes (and vice versa), display letters are different animals, designed for different purposes. As far back as Imperial Rome, sign painters and stone carvers employed lettering styles separate from the cursive and book hands of scribes. The classical capital letters carved into Roman edifices convey highly formalized elegance and detailing that match their monumental application. Since display letters mean to call attention to themselves, often at large sizes, designers creating display lettering or type have invented many ornamental and wildly unorthodox styles and treatments over the centuries.

Display lettering is found in posters, signs, web banners, magazine headlines, logos, graffiti, and countless other applications where the letters themselves must attract notice or convey an idea. Like book type and writing, display lettering is meant to be read, but display letters also set the visual and intellectual stage for the text's content. An uninflected sans serif headline in all caps might impart a modernist or rational feeling to a poster, while the same headline created with ornate, decorative letters could add a sense of obsession, opulence, or fussiness. Understanding such associations allows designers, letterers, and typographers to harness them to convey very specific moods and ideas using only the alphabet.

Good Stories
Magazine, 1899
The highly ornamented lettering on this masthead tells a story of its own. Functional serif book type is used for the small text, contrasting with the dominant display lettering to produce a visual hierarchy.

Freight Big
Freight Text
Typefaces, 2005
Joshua Darden

Refinements in stroke weight, contrast, and serif detailing differentiate the display font, Freight Big (shown solid here), from Freight's text weight (shown in outline).

Below:
Money #1
Hand-painted sign, 2002
Steve Powers
Artist Steve Powers uses the visual language and display lettering styles of twentieth-century signage to reinterpret anonymous consumerism into a series of personal messages.

Right:
An Albatross
Poster, 2004
Seripop
Gratuitous swashes were a common feature of 1970s display typography. On this poster excessive swashes mutate and sprout like kudzu throughout the hand-lettered text.

RKM52

Bell Centennial
Typeface, 1978
Matthew Carter
The ink traps and detailing added to improve the reproduction of very small text in telephone books become distinctive, ornamental elements at display sizes.

THIRTY PT
Thirty pt.
Thirty

EIGHT POINT UNITED SANS STENCIL
Eight point Interstate Thin Condensed
Eight point Bodoni No.1

ROGUES GALLERY
The characteristics that make display letters appropriate for use at large sizes make them poorly suited for small text. Subtle details and ornamentation disappear, while tight letterspacing that looks good large causes small type to seem cramped.

Display letters can be serif or sans serif, wide or narrow, ultra bold or ultra thin, extremely ornamental or uncompromisingly minimal. Hand-drawn lettering, scrawled characters, type, and even sculptural forms built as furniture or shaped from food can function as display. A wide range of possibilities and parameters exists for display lettering, constricted only by a project's demands and the designer's creativity.

Typographic conventions bend farther with display lettering than with book type. Where book type must maintain basic levels of legibility to stay useful, display lettering can conform more readily to a designer's or letterer's creative impulses, design parameters, or conceptual system. Designers may feel freer to push the boundaries of legibility, especially with very short amounts of text. In certain cases it is justifiable or even desirable to make readers exert themselves to decipher the content. Like a couture gown, specific display letters might not be appropriate for all situations, but they can convey a dramatic first impression when used judiciously.

Letterers and typographers frequently create hierarchy by mixing display letters with book type. A poster that screams JAMES BROWN with ultra bold in-your-face letters catches the viewer's eye. After drawing the viewer in with arresting display type, smaller book type assumes the more mundane task of announcing where to buy concert tickets. Since display type is less adaptable and less useful at small sizes, such partnerships between display and book letters allow compromises between typographic eye candy and legible functionality. Designers occasionally use book type at display sizes (generally above twelve points) to maintain consistency with body text or to emphasize subtle design features not apparent at text size. Fonts like Matthew Carter's Bell Centennial or John Downer's Vendetta reveal unorthodox detailing and construction when blown up large.

Book type adapted for display purposes conveys a very different spirit from that of letters made from jewelry, hotdogs, or toys. Display lettering's ability to employ any number of materials, attitudes, and techniques has given rise to an ever-growing body of letter styles, conceptual alphabets, and inventive approaches. Designers and artists continue to explore the possibilities of the alphabet, and their letters speak with an endless variety of voices and tones.

Dishwasher Pete

May 24th / 7pm / Atomic POP

3050 Falls Rd. Baltimore / 410.662.4444 / www.atomicbooks.com

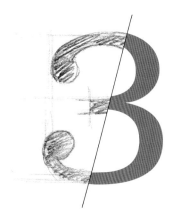

CREATING LETTERS

THINKING BEFORE DRAWING

No successful typeface or lettering treatment just *happens*. Before the pencils are sharpened or the computer screen illuminated, there is an idea or concept. A designer understands the content that the letters will communicate and the context in which they will appear. The clearer this perception is, the more precise and powerful are the project's results. A well-developed idea contributes just as much as well-constructed characters to lettering and type's successful outcome.

Letters are never neutral no matter how "neutral" they may look. Every style and approach is weighted with its unique baggage. Neutrality itself, a trait often praised in Helvetica and other modernist types, carries somewhat conflicting associations of both intellectuality and blandness. The abstract nature of letters affords them physical flexibility but also opens them to the burden of countless subjective associations. Designers can summon a variety of strikingly different voices from the exact same text simply by adjusting the letters' appearance. The visual elements of letters (style, scale, color, and the like) combine with these numerous contextual associations to establish tone.

A designer's understanding of such associations is just as important as a firm command of the alphabet's forms. Designers consciously choose styles whose contextual relationships best complement, illuminate, or expand on the content. Letters can work in concert with imagery. Pairing spare modernist type with a photo of minimalist architecture reinforces the associations of both the text and the image. Pairing elaborate, hand-drawn lettering with the same photo creates contrast and an entirely different set of associations. Since type or lettering can communicate a very specific perspective or tone, a grasp of these relationships is as crucial as a designer's drawing skill.

PARTY
Party
PARTY

Disparate styles of letters add their own color and connotations to text. Each of these three lettering treatments suggests a very different kind of party.

Dishwasher Pete
Poster, 2007
Oliver Munday
Under-the-sink water pipes become the initials of Dishwasher Pete, an itinerant author who spent more than a decade attempting to hold down dishwashing jobs in every state in America.

City of Brotherly Love

Ambigram, 2000

John Langdon

Ambigrams exploit the flexibility of letterforms to present words that can be read from multiple orientations. Intensive planning and sketching are required to make the same combination of strokes (in "Love" and "City of Brotherly/Philadelphia") describe multiple, dissimilar characters, from different viewpoints.

Articulate

Editorial illustration sketch, 2007

Post Typography

Thorny barbs added to a calligrapher's cartouche cause the word to take on a darker, less-positive significance.

Luke Moore bangs three

Luke Moore bangs thre

Luke Moore bangs t

'Fame is not all it is made o

'I have a job to do-we ar

Three face jail over M

DOES SPELLING REALLY MATTER? AS Molesworth might have observed, any fule kno it don't. Tony Blair wrote "toomorrow" three times in a memo, Keats once spelled fruit as "furuit", Yeats wrote peculiarities as "peculeraritys", and Hemingway wrote professional as "proffessional". Clearly such mistakes may not help you to be topp in skool, but

DOES SPELLING REALLY MATTER? AS Molesworth might have observed, any fule kno it don't. Tony Blair wrote "toomorrow" three times in a memo, Keats once spelled fruit as "furuit", Yeats wrote peculiarities as "peculeraritys", and Hemingway wrote professional as "proffessional". Clearly such mistakes may not help you to be topp in skool, but

Guardian Egyptian

Type family, 2005

Paul Barnes and Christian Schwartz

England's the Guardian commissioned this extensive, proprietary font family for use in the pages of its newspaper and magazine. Barnes and Schwartz developed multiple styles of Guardian Egyptian for diverse applications, including condensed fonts that allowed for longer headlines and versions adapted for very small text. Several slight weight variations (or grades) were created to account for ink spread on different paper stocks and presses.

THE LETTERING PROCESS

Very few people can jump into a typeface design or lettering treatment and produce a perfect set of letters in one shot. Even lettering or handwriting that appears casual or off-the-cuff is usually the result of an extended process, which might involve quickly writing the same word dozens or hundreds of times until perfected. When creating lettering or type, designers often begin with pencil and paper to produce a quicker, more natural evolution that stays true to the designer's hand—even when the final letters are rendered digitally. Since the computer screen's crispness adds a polished facade to even poorly drawn characters, many letterers and type designers try to pin down the essence of their letterforms on paper before taking them into the computer.

All letters are not created in the exact same way, but common steps are at the heart of drawing letters for typefaces as well as custom lettering treatments. A designer's initial idea first appears in sketch form—as thumbnails in a notebook, a rough digital layout, or perhaps a doodle on a napkin. Typically, designers go through

The Deathset
Lettering sketches for CD cover, 2008
Nolen Strals
When creating hand-drawn lettering, designers typically start by drawing loose skeletons of the characters and layout to resolve proportions and spacing. The letters' outlines and relationships become gradually more defined with each step of the process.

2007 Johns Hopkins Film Festival
3-D poster, 2007
Post Typography

To harness the 3-D effect of anaglyphic printing, two drawings of slightly different perspectives mimic the left and right eyes' points of view. Based on initial sketches, a physical model of the "type tower" was built and photographed from two angles. These two photographs became reference images for the two final lettering treatments on the red and blue printing plates.

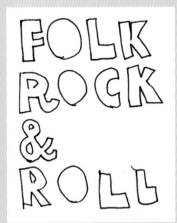
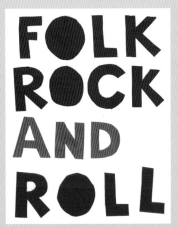

Folk Rock and Roll
Sketches and T-shirt graphic, 2007
Wyeth Hansen

The design process often leads down unintended paths. This lettering started as intentionally crude, analog forms, which mutated as Hansen began to experiment with quilting-inspired digital patterns. Unhappy with his initial computer-drawn results, Hansen redrew all of the artwork by hand before digitally rendering the final design.

multiple rounds of sketches in which they define and refine their letters' system and soul. Each ensuing sketch may be slightly more detailed and polished, as the designer resolves the letterforms and their relationships to each other. This process exposes flaws and conundrums, occasionally necessitating a return to square one—which is much easier to do with rough sketches than with detailed drawings. As the sketch reaches a certain level of refinement, the designer abandons looseness and makes the transition to a final medium or form, where the letters are inked, sculpted, cut, digitized, or otherwise completed.

This is by no means a fast process. Lettering is slow and meticulous work. Each step—conceiving, sketching, creating roughs, and finishing the artwork—can take hours, days, or weeks to complete. Designers and letterers labor even over thumbnails, honing the original design before embarking on the lengthy process of perfecting each letter's shape. The concept and sketch stages regularly take much longer than the final rendering. As each individual letter develops, every small adjustment is scrutinized for how it relates to its immediate neighbors and within the overall system. A word is more than the sum of its parts only if each letter acts purposefully.

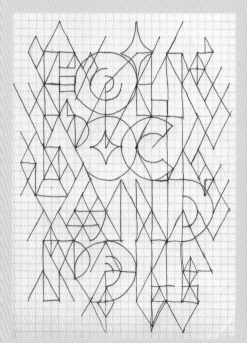

ANGLE OF TRANSLATION

The angle at which a flat-tipped writing tool is held determines the axis and stroke emphasis within letters. Strokes become thickest as they move perpendicular to the pen nib and thin as they move along the angle of the writing tip. The angle of translation informs the appropriate patterns of emphasis of any letter, whether drawn with a pen or constructed digitally.

FOUNDATIONS

The same basic principles shape all letters, whether a lighthearted typeface or an austere bespoke headline. Fundamentals of structure, proportion, and color determine legibility, even for letters that test its limits. The rules that guide letters can best be bent if they are first understood.

The lowercase characters of the alphabet are the most widely used and read. Their basic anatomy derives from centuries of letters written with a broad-nibbed pen. This flat-tipped writing tool creates areas of thicks and thins within each character, building a pattern of contrasting emphasis that continues throughout the alphabet. The historical source for capital letters is different, but the pens, brushes, and chisels used to make their classical forms reflect the same pattern of stroke modulation.

Modulation creates the axis of a letter, the angle of emphasis visible in rounded letters like the O. Through thousands of years of reading and repetition, the Western eye has grown accustomed to the pen-drawn form of the alphabet and its slightly sloped or vertical axis. The generally vertical stress of the pen is the reason why letters' horizontal strokes are thinner than their verticals, even in low-contrast sans serifs.

Awareness of axis and the pen's emphasis provides a key for understanding the shapes of the roman alphabet. A letter with no stroke modulation or whose horizontal strokes are thicker than its verticals will look wrong to the reader. Occasionally designers use such wrongness to great effect, but more frequently it betrays a poorly constructed character.

The relationships and dimensions of individual elements within each letter establish its proportions. Proper proportioning determines a letter's stability, tone, and legibility, and tells whether it is cut from the same cloth as its neighbors. The white space inside and around letters (the negative space) is as important as the marks that define a letter's structure: altering the proportions of an R's three negative spaces, for example, can dramatically change the properties and appearance of the letterform. The space between characters in a word also affects how the text is perceived. Since the eye primarily recognizes the outlines of letters, minimizing the space between characters reduces legibility. Conversely, excessive or irregular spacing maroons letters in a sea of white, disrupting the flow of reading.

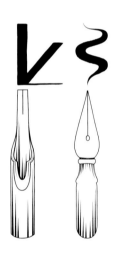

A broad-nibbed pen's stroke weight varies according to the width of the flat nib and the stroke's angle of translation. The stroke weight of an expandable nib depends on the pressure applied by the writer more than the angle of the hand holding the pen. The popularization of expandable nibs influenced type and calligraphy styles of the eighteenth century.

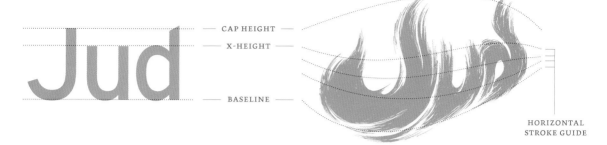

CAP HEIGHT
X-HEIGHT
BASELINE

HORIZONTAL
STROKE GUIDE

Although lettering and type design are two distinct practices, they share many of the same structural foundations. The invisible guidelines of the cap height, x-height, and baseline help determine the consistency and personality of both lettering and type.

If the baseline and cap height of the word shape fluctuate, counter spaces and stroke weights change in proportion to the overall size and shape of the letters. A varied stroke weight emphasizes the spatial quality of characters drawn in perspective.

Even when creating broken or ornamental letters, designers will make decisions that suggest the traditional forms of the characters. Decorative forms and breaks in stencil letters typically relate to norms of stroke axis, modulation, and serif placement.

Words on a curve or angle look and read best when the shape of the baseline reverberates upward through the entire structure of the characters.

ROGUES GALLERY
Curving or bending type digitally destroys the stroke proportions and detailing of the original letters. Redrawing the characters manually enables the designer to finesse and preserve the traits of the letterforms.

The "color" of type or lettering is the overall lightness or darkness of its letters. In the pages of this book, the paragraphs all have a consistent visual color across them. No characters appear significantly darker or lighter than others. The letters of the typeface work in unison, each stroke, counter, and letterspace balancing to create a cohesive rhythm. The more a particular letter stands out from its neighbors in shape, size, or color, the quicker a reader's eye is drawn to and gets stuck on it. Cohesiveness makes text easier to read; a letter that interrupts the eye is a visual roadblock that breaks readability.

The underlying principles and origins of the alphabet affect the way we perceive letterforms, from letters that invoke historical conventions to those that follow an unorthodox path. Though the processes and goals differ for each designer—whether creating lettering, writing, or type—the same concerns and relationships apply to any kind of letter.

EXERCISE: FLAT-TIPPED PEN

The contemporary shapes of the roman alphabet developed from calligraphic forms written with a flat-tipped, broad-nibbed pen. Even highly rationalized letterforms and typefaces are interpretations of these organic, handwritten shapes. Traces of the broad-nibbed pen live on in almost every typeface as modulated stroke weights and thick or thin axes.

Using a flat-tipped calligraphy pen or sharpened carpenter's pencil, practice drawing the alphabet on these pages. The hand holding the pen

Begin by drawing these basic strokes, taking care to hold the pen at a constant angle. Use the entire forearm more than the wrist. Repeatedly draw these basic strokes until they are fluent and consistent.

Letters are formed with combinations of strokes. The first stroke defines the character's width, height, and placement, while additional strokes complete its proportions and form. Practice drawing the alphabet until the proportions and construction of the letterforms start to feel smooth and natural.

should be kept at a relatively consistent angle throughout the stroke; a thirty-degree angle creates the forms shown here. Changing the angle of the pen changes the axis of the stroke. Held horizontally, the pen creates a modern axis with highly contrasting vertical and horizontal strokes. Compare these pen-lettered forms to typefaces like Jenson, Garamond, and Baskerville, noting the relationships in axis, emphasis, stroke weight, and serif construction. Almost all typefaces are informed by these hand-drawn origins, paying homage to them in different ways. Even sans serifs like Franklin Gothic and Gill Sans retain subtle traces of the pen in their letterforms.

Since the uppercase have evolved from lettered rather than handwritten forms, capital letters are built more geometrically than lowercase ones. With the exception of the Zs and some serifs, the angle of the pen stays consistent in humanist calligraphy.

To learn more about the art of calligraphy see Sheila Waters's Foundations of Calligraphy (Greensboro, NC: John Neal Bookseller, 2006).

PEN LETTERING BY CARA DI EDWARDO

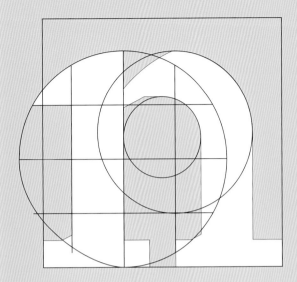

nerkotsy|

migf ɪzxv

sure

Under the guise of night, my trusty mate

PROSTHETICS

SEDENTARY INDIVIDUALS AROSE ONCE

Monarchs withheld municipal records for an

2198450

Does the rest of your team want water?

Reactive agents

Vendetta
Typeface, 1999
John Downer, Emigre
Vendetta employs an unusual construction that is both calli-graphic and geometric. The letters' abundant facets and angular strokes become apparent when shown at display sizes.

dagen

dagen

dagen

dagen

Type design is done
by specialists called type designers.
At least, that's what we may think at first.

Versa
Drawings and typeface, 1993–2004
Peter Verheul, OurType
Versa's organic forms were originally conceived as a display alphabet, following in the footsteps of faces like Albertus and Optima. As Verheul refined the typeface, its original eccentricities became less pronounced, and the final roman exhibits the evenness and openness of text type.

News
Magazine
BANNER

Magazine
DISPLAY

Magazine
SUBHEAD

Magazine
TEXT

Magazine
PLUS

Magazin
REVERSE

Vincent
Type family, 1999
Matthew Carter
*Commissioned as a type family
for* Newsweek *magazine,
Vincent's six fonts are each
designed for specific applications. The display faces have
narrower widths and spacing,
while two text weights provide
slight variations in overall
color. The heavier Reverse
is used for setting white
text knocked out of a dark
background.*

CREATING TEXT LETTERS AND BOOK TYPE

Reading a good book typeface is like wearing a well-broken-in shoe. The eye slips comfortably into the letters, which become an extension of the text itself. To maintain this comfortable and transparent quality, the shapes of book letters cannot stray too far from the conventions of legibility. Even the most contemporary and imaginative text type is part of a long visual lineage. Any letter whose form departs too far from the currently accepted shapes of the roman alphabet will be more difficult to read, especially at small sizes and for large bodies of text. Nonetheless, designers have managed to interpret book writing, lettering, and typography in expansive ways.

Creating text type is an arcane craft that is fundamentally bound to perceptions of legibility and readability. For most of alphabetic history, all letters were created at actual size. Contemporary designers enjoy the relatively recent luxury of working in large dimensions and scaling their letters at will. Although working at actual size leaves less room both for error and for delicate detailing, it provides a direct connection to the letters' end use. Like telecommuting to a job, working large offers countless benefits, but it can also leave a designer isolated and out of touch. For type designers working digitally, or otherwise scaling lettering or handwriting, the context of end use is crucial—they must constantly keep in mind how the characters will appear in their intended environment. Letters that look great six inches high may look terrible when used at book sizes.

Since all metal type is created at actual size, designers of metal type must create separate matrices for each point size of a typeface. Although this is a much more arduous task than repurposing a single font for many sizes, it allows a type designer to optimize each letter for its end use. As the font sizes grow smaller, a type designer will subtly increase the x-height, letterspacing, and width while exaggerating small details like serifs and aperture size. Contrast generally decreases at small sizes, to maintain the robustness of thin strokes. Even though these adjustments may slightly alter the character of the letterforms, they make letters more legible and readable at small sizes. Some contemporary designers and digital type foundries have revived the practice of releasing typefaces with multiple fonts for specific sizes, acknowledging that type designed for use at twelve point may not work as well at six point.

Reading a good book typeface is like wearing a well-broken-in shoe. The eye slips comfortably into the letters, which become an extension of the text itself. To maintain this comfortable and transparent quality, the shapes of book letters cannot stray too far from the conventions of legibility. Even the most contemporary and imaginative text

Reading a good book typeface is like wearing a well-broken-in shoe. The eye slips comfortably into the letters, which become an extension of the text itself. To maintain this comfortable and transparent quality, the shapes of book letters cannot stray too far from the conventions of legibility. Even the most

Reading a good book typeface is like wearing a well-broken-in shoe. The eye slips comfortably into the letters, which become an extension of the text itself. To maintain this comfortable and transparent quality, the shapes of book letters cannot stray too far from the conventions of legibility. Even the most contemporary and

Reading a good book typeface is like wearing a well-broken-in shoe. The eye slips comfortably into the letters, which become an extension of the text itself. To maintain this comfortable and transparent quality, the shapes of book letters cannot stray too far from the conventions of legibility. Even the most contemporary and imaginative

Reading a good book typeface is like wearing a well-broken-in shoe. The eye slips comfortably into the letters, which become an extension of the text itself. To maintain this comfortable and transparent quality, the shapes of book letters cannot stray too far from the conventions of legibility. Even the

Reading a good book typeface is like wearing a well-broken-in shoe. The eye slips comfortably into the letters, which become an extension of the text itself. To maintain this comfortable and transparent quality, the shapes of book letters cannot stray too far from the conventions of legibility. Even

Reading a good book typeface is like wearing a well-broken-in shoe. The eye slips comfortably into the letters, which become an extension of the text itself. To maintain this comfortable and transparent quality, the shapes of book letters cannot stray too far from the conventions of legibility. Even the most contemporary and imaginative text type is

Reading a good book typeface is like wearing a well-broken-in shoe. The eye slips comfortably into the letters, which become an extension of the text itself. To maintain this comfortable and transparent quality, the shapes of book letters cannot stray too far from the conventions of legibility. Even the most contemporary and

1. Walter Tracy, *Letters of Credit* (Boston: David R. Godine, Publisher, 1986), chap. 7.

While all text type aspires to certain standards of legibility and readability, fonts that can perform at text sizes come in many different styles and flavors.

While the basic frames of the roman alphabet forms cannot be distorted too much without damaging their legibility, the details that give letters their personality are malleable and subject to numerous interpretations. Walter Tracy, in his book *Letters of Credit*, lists three principal elements that define the individuality of book type.[1] *Stroke weight* and *contrast* are the heaviness of the line and the amount of variation between thick and thin—a high-contrast V may pair a heavy left stroke with a very fine right diagonal. *Axis* or *stress* alludes to the pen's angle of translation and determines where the heaviest part of a round stroke falls—the O of a modern letter is heaviest on its left and right sides, while a humanist O's weight is distributed more toward its northeast and southwest corners. *Serif shape* is defined by the designer and relates to the overall tone and origins of a letter's style.

Although contrast, axis, and serif shape are crucial to classifying and categorizing letters, several other factors are also important to the overall spirit and legibility of text letters. The *x-height* and the length of *ascenders* and *descenders* critically affect a letter's legibility, readability, and proportions—long ascenders and descenders look elegant and improve the readability of wordshapes, but they inversely affect the x-height and legibility at small sizes. *Aperture*—the size of the openings in letters like C or a—is another factor in legibility. The *shape* and *geometry of curves* also influence letters, since the framework of book letters depends on the curves of the lowercase alphabet—round, generous curves might make letters feel open and friendly, while other angles can suggest the trace of the pen. Perhaps most subtle but no less important, *line* and *edge quality* affects a letter's general tone and expression. Lines can feel soft and supple, straight and precise, faceted, or even rough and textured. Line quality is less apparent at small sizes, but its nuances contribute to the overall feel of the lettering, writing, or type.

These essential elements—contrast, axis, serifs (if any), curve shape, x-height, aperture, and line quality—blend with many other specific decisions and individual characteristics to give text letters their own voice. Any of these elements can be taken to extremes, but doing so will affect the letter's legibility or the text's readability. Designers of book and text letters delicately blend form and function within the basic framework of the alphabet and the confines of legibility.

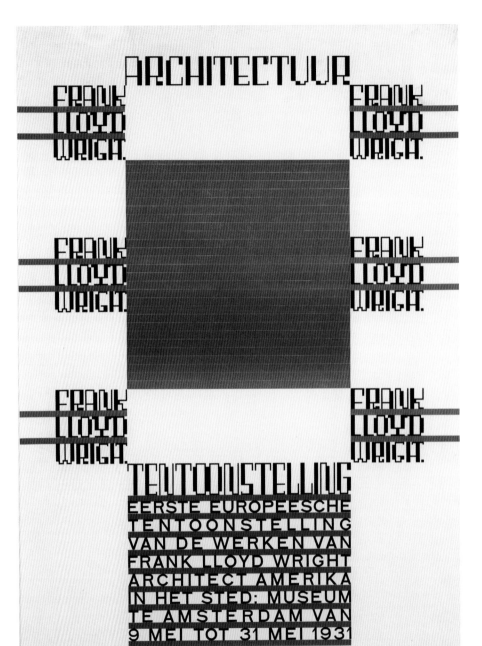

ARCHITECTUUR

FRANK LLOYD WRIGH.

FRANK LLOYD WRIGH.

FRANK LLOYD WRIGH.

FRANK LLOYD WRIGH.

FRANK LLOYD WRIGH.

FRANK LLOYD WRIGH.

TENTOONSTELLING
EERSTE EUROPEESCHE
TENTOONSTELLING
VAN DE WERKEN VAN
FRANK LLOYD WRIGHT
ARCHITECT AMERIKA
IN HET STED: MUSEUM
TE AMSTERDAM VAN
9 MEI TOT 31 MEI 1931

DE TENTOONSTELLINGS
RAAD VOOR BOUWKUNST
EN VERWANTE KUNSTEN

JOH. ENSCHEDE EN ZONEN HAARLEM   H. TH. WIJDEVELD AMSTERDAM

MODULAR LETTERS

Modular describes any letter assembled from a limited palette of distinct elements. In one sense, almost all typefaces are modular—a font's system is usually built around a similar set of shapes and marks. But where most typefaces adjust their traits to suit each character's needs and structure, modular letters follow a strict system with a fixed set of modules. Typically these elements are geometric and simple in shape— square pixels on a digital display or modernist circles, squares, and lines—but designers are increasingly using more ornate forms and even physical objects to construct modular letters.

Traditionally, modular lettering has responded to the limitations and possibilities of the media used to create it. Avant-garde designers in the early twentieth century used decorative, geometric elements from the letterpress to build modular letterforms. Their work explored and celebrated the grid, a trend also seen in the modern art and architecture of their contemporaries. Expanding and exploiting the abstract nature of the alphabet, these designers approached letters as structural rather than handwritten forms.

Contemporary designers have taken a broader approach to modular letterforms, pushing the possibilities of digital screen fonts and creating letters from more complicated elements. Modular letters force the designer to work within a strict system, a limit that many designers find a compelling challenge as they manipulate predetermined elements in new ways. Although the components of modular lettering are limited, the spirit and shapes of the letters themselves are not.

Frank Lloyd Wright Architecture Exhibition
Poster, 1931
Hendrik Theodorus Wijdeveld
This poster's headline text is constructed from ornamental printers' rules and letterpress blocks.
Minneapolis Institute of Arts, The Modernism Collection, gift of Norwest Bank Minnesota.

Arrays of physical objects, such as the bricks of this London market's facade, can become elements for making letterforms.
Photo by Daniel Rhatigan.

Electronic signboards and monitors use modular grids to display information. This sign's grid is surprisingly complex, as revealed by the malfunctioning E.

Above:

Young Leader Live Sessions

Lettering, 2004

Alex Trochut

Although sinuous and decorative in appearance, the characters in this lettering treatment are assembled from a reduced set of elements.

Below:

Scandinavian Sparks

Typeface, 2004

Hjärta Smärta

Created for an exhibition of Swedish art and design, the characters of Scandinavian Sparks are built from symbols and motifs found in traditional Swedish handicrafts.

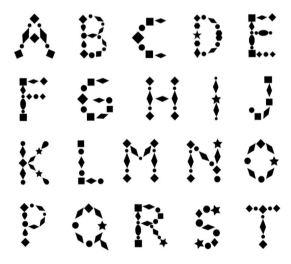

Whimcircle

Alphabet, 2004

Tore Terrasi

EXERCISE: MODULAR ALPHABET

From modernist experiments to bitmap fonts, designers have explored the possibilities of creating letters from a reduced palette of shapes. The predefined forms and restrictive systems of modular letters make them a quick and approachable method for building letters. In spite of the constraints, new and surprising letterforms can be built with modular elements.

Create an alphabet using only a small set of basic geometric shapes. Begin by working on a grid, where the regular and repetitive modular elements feel most at home. Your grid can be reductive, expansive, or somewhere in between. After establishing a grid and a visual approach, design letters that represent the alphabet's basic forms like H, O, M, R, A, or n, o, b, a, v. Stick to and refine the system as needed, until these initial letterforms feel consistent. Gradually construct more characters until you have designed the entire alphabet. Test the letters in word combinations periodically to expose flaws and inconsistencies.

Maintaining equal widths and proportions, build a modular alphabet from these three geometric shapes: a 1x1 square, a 1x2 rectangle, and a 1x1 quarter circle. Use as many or few shapes as needed. Bear in mind that smaller grids provide a more limited set of design options.

Keep the shapes proportional; do not scale or distort any of the components. Do not overlap the elements or use a white shape knocked out of black forms.

Examples of student work from the Maryland Institute College of Art

KATIE MCLACHLAN

KATE MORGAN

CARLOS VIGIL

EUGENIA WANG

EMIGRE

heritage

No.14/$7.95

SCREEN FONTS

The limitations of digital technology present a different kind of challenge for type designers. Some electronic displays force the rounded and irregular forms of the alphabet to conform to their pixel grid. Screen and bitmap fonts are modular typefaces designed specifically for display on digital screens. These faces use the smallest element of the display, usually pixels or LEDs, as their module. When enlarged, bitmap forms appear blocky and jagged, but at small sizes a well-designed bitmap font can suggest the subtleties and curves possessed by analog typefaces. Designers of bitmap fonts have tackled the difficult problems of making screen type legible at small sizes and converting the nuances of a serif typeface into chunky pixel modules. Some designers use the limitations of bitmap fonts for visual effect, blowing them up to large sizes, building ornate forms from pixels, or incongruously using screen fonts for print applications.

Emigre #14
Magazine cover, 1990
Rudy VanderLans
This issue of the design magazine Emigre examines the impact of Switzerland's design heritage on young Swiss designers. Its cover combines old and new in lettering, rendering pen-derived Fraktur letters as digital bitmaps.

WHEN ENLARGED, BITMAP FORMS APPEAR BLOCKY AND JAGGED, BUT AT SMALL SIZES A WELL-DESIGNED BITMAP FONT CAN SUGGEST THE SUBTLETIES AND CURVES POSSESSED BY ANALOG TYPEFACES. Designers of bitmap fonts have tackled the difficult problem of making screen type legible at small sizes, or converting the nuances of a serif typeface into chunky pixel modules.

FFF Alias
Seven-pixel typeface, 2002
Fonts For Flash

For more on the complex processes of adapting type for the screen, see the Microsoft Typography Group: www.microsoft.com/typography.

rotfl 1337
rotfl 1337
ROTFL 1337
rotfl 1337
rotfl 1337

Unibody
Eight-pixel typeface, 2003
Underware
Unibody is a surprisingly typographic family of bitmap fonts. By altering the emphasis of the letters' "curves," its italic creates the appearance of sloped forms without actually slanting the letters.

g g g
Georgia
Georgia
Georgia

Georgia
Typeface, 1996
Matthew Carter, Tom Rickner
The nuances of a scalable, vector typeface designed for print do not always translate well to the screen. Anti-aliasing is a method of suggesting curves by blurring and graying the ragged edges of the bitmaps. When designing Georgia for Microsoft, Carter worked in reverse of the typical process, beginning with a bitmap version of the fonts, which were then adapted into the more refined outline version.

TIME

SPECIAL Edition

The TIME

100

the
MOST
Influential
People in the
World

A NOVE
A NOVEL
A NOVEL
A NOVEL
A NOVEL
A NOVEL
A NOVEL
A NOVEL

Because of the spontaneity and variable qualities of handwriting, designers will often write the same text several or even dozens of times, until the right balance of form, personality, and legibility is achieved.

Opposite:
100 Most Influential People
Magazine cover, 2008
James Victore
Quickly executed handwriting, enlarged to display size, creates a striking contrast with the rectangular border and precisely rendered forms of the Time masthead.

Right:
Baxter
Typeface, 2006
Tal Leming and Christian Schwartz
Baxter translates the friendly, careful forms of schoolbook handwriting into type. Although it bypasses some of handwriting's inconsistencies for the sake of a cohesive system, this typeface maintains a spontaneous spirit.

This letter from 1908 shows an elegant script written with a flexible-nibbed pen. Before the widespread use of typewriters and computers, handwriting expertise was considered an important social and business skill.

HANDWRITING

Handwriting is the simplest form of creating letters and has existed parallel to lettering since the beginning of the alphabet. Handwritten letters are typically made with one or two quick and fluid marks. Although some lettering is also drawn with a few simple lines, the intent of the writer separates writing from lettering. Handwriting is usually more casual and efficient than lettering. Where lettering is mainly concerned with the visual appearance of the text, writing focuses on putting information quickly to page.

This emphasis on speed and function does not preclude writing from speaking in its own visual tongue. Handwriting can convey the delicacy and sophistication of a formal cursive, the relaxed timbre of a quick note, or the shakiness of a lunatic scrawl. When written deliberately, handwriting operates much like a palette of fonts. Slight variations in style can express different tones while maintaining the consistency of the writer's hand. Although lettering and type can also evoke personality and mood, handwriting adds an intimacy that the others cannot. Graphologists and other handwriting analysts believe that handwriting can subconsciously reveal a person's mental or physical state.

Cursives, romans, quickly written capitals, and even combinations of the three can be examples of handwriting. Script and cursive styles are a common form of handwriting, since connecting multiple letterforms with a continuous line increases writing speed. Writing naturally expresses both the hand of its writer and the tool used to create it, whether a crayon, pencil, or broad-nibbed pen. The expressive and personal qualities inherent in handwriting have given it added significance in a world of precise and often impersonal digital type.

Robin Hood saves the day
NOTTINGHAM
Quality porridge admirers
BEAR FAMILY

SILLY SPIDER
Unprepared for downpour
TOADSTOOLS
King Toad taunts subjects

SCRIPT LETTERING

Script lettering translates the sinuous italic forms of cursive writing into a more formal system. When most people think of scripts they imagine the classic, slightly embellished wedding invitation styles popularized by calligraphy textbooks and numerous digital typefaces. But scripts comprise a surprisingly broad range of approaches, from sloppy brush lettering to pixel fonts to elegant formal calligraphy. Some scripts are even streamlined and geometric, such as the mechanical scripts that embodied the Art Deco style of the 1920s and 1930s. The defining characteristic of script lettering or type is a visual link to the flowing forms of hand-drawn cursives.

Where handwriting strives for speed and utility, script lettering is more methodically and purposefully executed. Although many scripts give the appearance of a fluid line of spontaneously written text, the characters are often built from many strokes or processes. Digital lettering treatments and typefaces that mimic the flowing forms of the brush or pen require a particularly complex process to translate smooth cursives into the mathematical realm of the computer. The most accomplished script lettering and typefaces convincingly reproduce the effortless motion of calligraphy, even when the letters are laboriously or geometrically constructed. Some of these brush scripts and calligraphic lettering evolve like a movie—the final version edits together the best letters from multiple takes.

Digital technology has essentially eliminated cursive handwriting from everyday communication, and a lack of regular exposure to script and cursive letters makes these one of the more difficult styles for many contemporary designers to master. Yet the same absence from the visual environment gives scripts, especially custom lettering, a visual singularity that can bridge the gap between type and handwriting.

Universal Penman (detail)
Calligraphy sample book, 1743
George Bickham, based on lettering by J. Champion
The elegant scripts in this famous English penmanship guidebook were meant to serve as practical examples for formal business and correspondence writing.

1. CORPUS, Editorial lettering, 2007, Apirat Infahseng
2. MOLOTOV, Logo, 2008, Andy Cruz and Eric Marcinizyn
3. FIG SCRIPT, Typeface, 2001–2002, Process Type Foundry
4. REALITY IS NOT CONTROLLABLE, Editorial Lettering, 2007, Damien Correll
5. IS NOT MAGAZINE, Logo, 2005, Underware
6. EMIGRE, Logo, 2004, John Downer
7. KANT, Logo, 2007, Underware
8. UNITING, Lettering, 2006, Topos Graphics
9. SUSANNAH, Logo, 2004, Underware
10. POP ART, Logo, 2000, House Industries

corpus!

1

Molotov

2

Picturesque

3

Reality is not Controllable

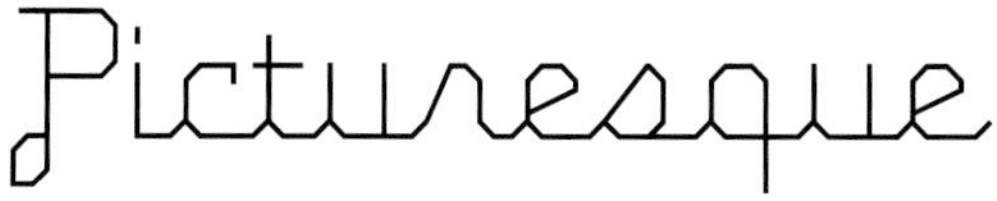

4

Is Not Magazine

5

Emigre

6

KANT

7

Uniting

8

Susannah

9

Popart

10

CASUAL LETTERING

Casual letters do not take themselves too seriously. These spontaneous-feeling styles encompass brush scripts, whimsical handwriting, and the animated bounciness of cartoon lettering. The forms can be lively cursives or chunky block letters, hairline thin or obese, serif or sans, sitting on a solid baseline or bouncing, overlapped or interlocked. Casual lettering often displays a naive or anarchic quality, meant to give the impression that the letterforms were rapidly thrown together, whether or not this is the case. Their general lack of sobriety and formality gives casual letters a license to break rules of proportion and position, rejecting the rigidity of conventional typography in favor of liveliness and personality.

A whimsical offshoot of signage and advertising styles, casual lettering arose at the beginning of the twentieth century alongside comic strips, vaudeville, and ragtime music. Hand-painted or -drawn casual lettering once graced sheet music, signage, packaging, and advertising of every stripe—on barbershops, cereal boxes, concert posters, and almost everything else. As digital typography replaced lettering in the late twentieth century, the use of casual lettering declined. The rigidity and impersonal qualities of type are contrary to the nature of casual lettering. Today, graphic designers frequently use fonts that impersonate casual lettering, but few of these typographic counterfeits achieve the same spirited quality, and their application is too often relegated to retro pastiche. As hand lettering has made a comeback in design, casual letters and their influence have returned to the mainstream, and more designers are approaching casual lettering in a contemporary way.

Casual lettering's spontaneous quirks often help letters interact with their neighbors. Bouncy letters create a rhythm that guides the eye through an otherwise unbalanced word. Interlocking letters poke at and bump around each other, fitting together like a jigsaw puzzle. A level of randomness in their application keeps these modifications from feeling forced and systematic. Casual lettering is an antidote to stiff and solemn typography.

Opposite:
Mighty Night
Flyer, 2007
Letman (Job Wouters)
Approachable hand lettering unites the dozens of casual styles on this poster.

You'll Find This A Very Good Book

Hand-drawn lettering, c. 1963

Shag Lounge and Burbank
Typefaces, 2003 and 2007
Tal Leming, House Industries
These typefaces pay homage to casual lettering of the mid-twentieth century. While type cannot duplicate all of the quirkiness and singularity of hand-drawn lettering, these fonts include alternate characters and ligatures that emulate the spirit of lettering while maintaining the flexibility of type.

All Giggles and Guffaws
LAF'N'GAS
TH' NERVOUS REX
SO UPTIGHT

EFFORTLESS
Partygoers play cards
NEIGHBORHOOD
MR. FURLEY

DISTRESSED TYPE

Social Coma
Record insert, 1997
Mark McCoy
*Each word of these densely
textured liner notes was applied
with cracked rub-down transfer
letters and further degraded
through repeated photocopying.*

Distressed type is what happens when nice, clean letters from a good family get dirty, are roughed up, and begin breaking the rules. Distress appears in worn or chipped edges and rough textures or at the extreme in ripped, broken, and distorted forms. Distressed letters can convey many effects, from simulating lo-fi reproduction methods to suggesting aging and decay or even violence. Today, distorted typography is frequently associated with the "grunge" design style of the 1990s, but intentionally disfigured type has historic precedents.

Type foundries at the turn of the twentieth century responded to a renewed interest in antiquity by introducing Rugged typefaces, whose rough edges and crude forms mimicked the coarse results of antique printing. Irregular edges typified these fonts, and their italics bore the uneven appearance of hand lettering. The Ruggeds were usually more of a caricature than a true revival, clothing nineteenth-century letterforms in the rough trappings of antique production methods.

Mid-twentieth-century designers used distress as a way to add emotion to text. Tony Palladino's deftly ripped logo for Alfred Hitchcock's *Psycho*

ANIVERSARIO DEL BOMBARDEO A HIROSHIMA 6 de Agosto   ANNIVERSAIRE DU BOMBARDEMENT A HIROSHIMA 6 aout
ANNIVERSARY OF THE BOMBING OF HIROSHIMA   August 6

Edison

Pabst Old Style
Typeface, 1902
Edward M. Lewis (original
version by Frederick Goudy)
*Rough edges and slightly irregular
characters are key traits of early-
twentieth-century Rugged types.*

**Hiroshima / Anniversary of the
Bombing**
Poster, 1970
René Mederos
*This broken, distorted headline
expresses the devastation caused
by the atomic bomb dropped on
Hiroshima.*
Courtesy of Lincoln Cushing.

ROGUES GALLERY
*Fonts with built-in degradation
lack the chaos and randomness
of truly distressed letters. When
a degraded letter shows up
twice, looking exactly the same,
it doesn't look "damaged" as
much as "fake."*

ROGUES GALLERY
*Gritty textures masked onto
clean-edged digital type are
a patina rather than actual
distress.*

Night Terrors
Logo, 2006
Nolen Strals
*Digitally sliced and shattered
type reflects the hard-hitting
tactics of this roller derby team.*

typographically portrayed the torn psyche of the lead character. Crumpled and broken letters have amplified the message in everything from headache medicine ads to antiwar posters. Punk rock of the 1970s introduced popular culture to the lo-fi aesthetics of zines, homemade posters, and DIY typography. Photocopiers and mimeograph machines provided cheap, gritty reproduction for artists working with little to no budget. Punk designers and artists exploited the degrading effects of these machines on type and image to great effect. Their cut-and-paste compositions, degraded and dirtied through repeated copying, reflected the raw, urgent sounds of the music the artwork accompanied.

In the 1990s, type designers echoed the renewed popularity of punk music and aesthetics with typefaces that imitated punk's gritty, damaged typography. Most of these fonts are the typographic equivalent of pre-ripped jeans—distressed type always looks more natural when it reflects the actual processes that have broken it in. Type can have more to say (and sometimes just looks cooler) when it's not so perfect.

Lettering

studio lettering swing

Studio Lettering Sable	**House Spencerian**	**Amerikanische Badneß**	**Strictly Hey-Wake**
Typeface, 2008	Logo, 2004	Lettering, 2007	Logo, 2003
Studio Lettering Swing Alternates	**Ed Interlock** ("industries")	**Only Vegas**	**Superv**
Typeface, 2008	Typeface, 2004	Logo, 2002	Logo, 1997

INTERVIEW: KEN BARBER

Letterer and type designer Ken Barber has masterminded thousands of typefaces and lettering treatments as typography director at the independent type foundry House Industries. Among the wide variety of lettering styles in his portfolio, Barber's accomplished casual and script letters are perhaps his best known.

What makes a successful lettering treatment? The hallmark of lettering is its uniqueness, and successful work capitalizes on this aspect. Hand-drawn letters not only convey the content of a particular message but also have the potential to become the content itself. Beyond that, good lettering should ultimately demonstrate harmony of form, balancing positive and negative shapes while maintaining visual uniformity.

How does your approach differ between lettering and type design? Lettering offers a remarkable amount of flexibility in terms of letterform construction, since only specific letters interact directly with one another. Typographic forms, on the other hand, must work within a comparatively less accommodating system; this demands sensitivity to the variable context in which the characters will appear.

What are the challenges of adapting one-of-a-kind hand lettering to the systematized format of type? Although typography can be suggestive of lettering, it's hardly a substitute for the real thing. The act of drawing is a singular expression that can't be exactly duplicated. Capturing the gestural nuances and subtleties of a hand-drawn silhouette is a tall order in digital type. Nevertheless, with keen observation and clever engineering, typefaces can emulate some patterns and characteristics of lettering. The evolving capabilities of digital font formats can also help bridge the gap between lettering and typography.

What considerations make creating a script typeface different from designing a roman? While roman forms are visually linked by the negative space between them, the letters in a script must physically connect in any given sequence. How this is accomplished is perhaps the most important consideration of a script. Consequently, special attention must be given to the construction of joining letters.

Without giving up the colonel's famous secret recipe, can you offer any tips or tricks for creating successful script or casual letters? Though I can't reveal all eleven herbs and spices, there are a few essentials that script and casual hands can't do without. (1) No matter what sort of letter you're creating, clearly defining its purpose and application is indispensable. (2) Inform your design by investigating historical forms. Seemingly disparate sources can end up influencing a project. (3) Stick to the basics. The fundamentals of lettering have endured for a reason, and they still apply in most instances. Study the work of those who inspire you—if possible, find a mentor. Books and workshops are helpful, too, but they can't replace an expert's hands-on guidance. (4) Observe the lettering around you, and learn from it. (5) Practice, practice, practice. Even if you don't become a virtuoso with a pen or brush, pushing around some ink on paper goes a long way toward unlocking the secrets of successful script lettering.

Bats & Spiders!

Bats & Spiders
Lettering, 2008
Adam Okrasinski
Removing the curves of elegant script type creates this jagged digital cursive.

The Dilapidated Reanimated Expo
Logo and icons, 2006
Post Typography
For an art show exploring the reuse of vacant properties in Baltimore, this logo's fallen counter forms reincarnate as support icons, following the lead of the work in the exhibition.

Beatbots
Logo, 2008
Oliver Munday
With a handful of well-placed adjustments and additions, type can be transformed into illustrative lettering. This motley cast of characters reflects the mix of contributors to this web magazine and message board.

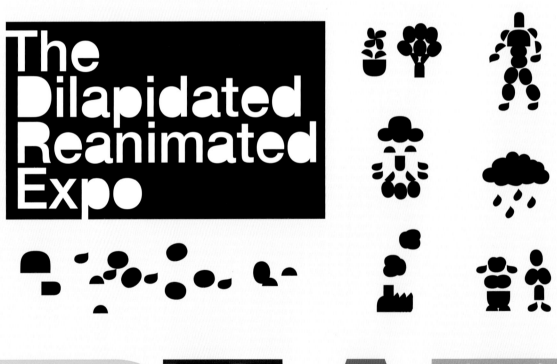

MAKING LETTERS WORK
TRANSFORMING TYPE

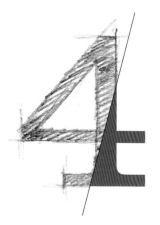

CUSTOMIZING TYPE

Customizing type gives prefab letters a new personality and individuality. Like a house or an apartment, letters can be built from the ground up, or preexisting structures can be decorated and modified to suit a designer's tastes and needs. Using existing type as a model or starting point is one common way that designers avoid the substantial investment needed for originally drawn lettering. Many lettering treatments begin with an existing typeface, either as inspiration or as raw material. Graphic designers alter type to achieve results that the original typeface cannot produce.

The rationales for customizing type are as varied as the alphabet itself. Modifying the characters of a logotype or headline text can give the letters new spirit or alter the tone and meaning of the original typography. Rounding the corners of one or two letters can make a cold word softer and more inviting. Adding swashes, flourishes, or ornamentation to a letterform can imbue it with new panache or delicacy. Joining two characters can imply connectedness or compactness. A subtle modification to a counterform or curve can provide an implicit connection to similarly shaped elements in a design. In some cases, an attribute or form that works well at small sizes may lose its attractiveness at large scale, demanding refinements or alterations.

Bryant **Bryant**
Bryant Bryant

Splice Today
Logo system, 2008
Post Typography

Bryant
Typeface, 2002–2005
Eric Olson, Process Type
Foundry
*A logotype that is based on an
existing font naturally shares
many of the font's traits,
making the original typeface
a natural companion to the
identity. Some designers take
this idea a step further by
creating or commissioning an
original, proprietary typeface
to better distinguish an organi-
zation's brand.*

Occasionally typographers create new or alternate characters to save a typeface from itself. Some otherwise useful fonts may lack a few essential characters, accents, or punctuation marks in their toolkit of symbols. At other times a typographer might find certain characters poorly drawn or unsuited to a particular need. Some less completely realized revivals of classical typefaces do not contain properly developed modern characters like the € (euro), @ (at symbol), and / \ (slashes). Since these symbols joined the typographic lexicon relatively recently, they are not in every typeface's original character set and may have been drawn with less regard or skill than the alphabet letters. Some fonts contain only tabular, lining numerals with unattractive text spacing, while others may have a letter that just feels out of place. Rather than settle for a typeface that is almost right, designers can create their own supplemental symbols, letters, or fonts to work alongside and enhance an existing typeface. Whether supplementing a font or turning type into lettering, customizing makes prefab letters speak with a new and individual voice.

TURNING TYPE INTO LETTERING

Designers alter type to create forms beyond the typical constraints of a font. Making these custom letters harmonize with their surroundings requires an understanding of the existing typographic system—how the new arrivals or adaptations interact with their neighbors is a chief concern. A designer usually attempts to integrate custom forms and modifications in a balanced way, although a jarring juxtaposition can sometimes produce striking effects. Respecting and paying attention to the relationships between modified characters and the system of their base typeface is the crucial factor in type customization.

Font Pirates and Saboteurs
Type design has a long and sordid history of piracy. Since the early days of movable type, rival foundries have created knockoffs and imitations of popular designs. As typography has migrated into digital formats, the means to copy, edit, and corrupt type have become relatively easy, leading to an increase in typeface forgeries and misguidedly altered fonts. While using type as a basis for lettering is a common practice, editing and changing the actual font itself is generally inadvisable and frequently illegal. Besides infringing on the type designer's copyright, a bastardized or altered typeface is rife with the technical and artistic problems that arise whenever a second (usually less skilled) author amends an original work.

WINGDINGS

ORIGINAL TYPE
(BODONI NO. 1 ITALIC)

UPRIGHT V ADDED,
SPACING ADJUSTED

LETTERS CONDENSED,
STROKE WEIGHT THINNED

NEW DOT ADDED TO i

Above:
Vic
Postcard, 2007
Post Typography
This logo for a jazz singer began as type, which was then customized to interact with an illustration.

CASE STUDY

ALL CAPS HELVETICA

case STUDY

LOWERCASE LETTERS INSERTED

case STUDY

A THINNER WEIGHT OF HELVETICA WITH A
COMPARABLE STROKE WEIGHT IS SUBSTITUTED

case STUDY

LOWERCASE CHARACTERS THICKENED TO
MATCH THE CAPITALS; SPACING IS ADJUSTED

Keeping It in the Family

Combining two styles, cases, or weights from the same family is one of the easiest ways to mix type. Since fonts in the same family share many of the same traits, the designer has fewer readjustments to make. This unicase lettering mixes lowercase characters with capitals, and a lighter weight of the font is adjusted to match the boldness of the uppercase.

ALTERED BEAST

ROGUES GALLERY

Since good fonts have a carefully defined system, customizations that disregard the attributes of the original typeface can create typographic monsters. Compensating for any changes that affect color, width, spacing, and consistency can help customized type atone for its sins.

Full Sail

FULL SAIL, Logo, 2005, Steve Sandstrom

STONE SOURCE

STONE SOURCE, Logo, 2008, Shaw Jelveh Design

RUSSIA!

RUSSIA! Logo, 2007, Art. Lebedev

MIXING FONTS, MIXING MESSAGES

Combining two different typefaces within the same word or the same line is the typographic equivalent of collage. Designers and typographers use this juxtaposition to create a variety of effects, from the sharp, sometimes shocking contrast between divergent faces to the subtle softening created by inserting a rounded lowercase form into a line of hard capital letters. While mash-ups of different fonts are relatively easy to execute, a successful mixture of typefaces requires finesse and attention to detail to merge dissimilar elements into a typographic whole.

1

2

3

4

5

6

7

8

9

10

11

12

13

14

15

For graphic designers creating logotypes, headlines, or other custom-lettering treatments, type is often a logical place to start. Customization adds singularity to off-the-shelf typography—an especially important approach for identities and editorial lettering.

Logotypes in particular demand a uniqueness that straight type may not provide. Simple and powerful type modifications are at the heart of many distinctive logos and lettering treatments.

EXERCISE: MODIFYING TYPE

Even minor adjustments can give type a new or more complex voice. An act as straightforward as rounding sharp corners or creating a stencil from a particular character can completely change the tone of a type treatment. Modifying an existing font shifts it from type into the realm of custom lettering, giving the letters their own unique flavor.

Choosing an existing typeface such as Helvetica, modify one word in several different ways to see how these alterations affect the appearance and tone of the letters. Pay careful attention to the type's underlying system. Modifications to one letter can affect the rest of the word in unforeseen ways and may require compensations in weight, spacing, and width. Any adjustments should respect the relationships of the typographic system.

LETTERING BY SARA FRANTZMAN

LIGATURES AND JOINED LETTERFORMS

Like musical ligatures that bind notes together, typographic ligatures are two or more characters joined to form a single glyph. In the days of metal type, ligatures were typically created when the spacing between irregularly shaped characters like the f or the y called for their forms to overlap or abut. Since the physical nature of lead type precludes such an overlap, metal typefaces required a separate glyph to combine the overlapping letters. Some contemporary typefaces have also revived archaic ligatures like ct that stemmed from handwritten sources.

The two most common typographic ligatures, fl and fi, are typically included in well-designed typefaces. The fl and fi glyphs, along with some rarer ligatures that join ty and ffl, address particular combinations of letters that cross paths or collide. Contemporary type designers increasingly include alternate, contextual, and decorative ligatures in their typefaces to give them more personality, flexibility, and customization options. Digital typography allows for large numbers of ligatures and alternates, granting new options for linking characters that are not possible with metal type. Script faces and other fonts that derive their forms from hand lettering benefit the most, since contextual ligatures can mimic elements of handwriting's irregularity and connectivity.

Custom lettering provides even more opportunities for connecting, overlapping, and locking letters together. Joining several characters can unify a word or logotype, converting it from a string of letters into an image or mark. Even with a proliferation of ligatures and alternates in type design, joined letterforms are still a hallmark of custom lettering. The juxtaposition of forms in a specific word may suggest new ligature combinations unavailable as type. With custom lettering, designers are not limited to a typical palette of ligatures or ones that connect only two adjacent characters. Even outlandish connections that stretch between words or snake around characters are fair game.

Catasticho
Manuscript, 1478–1520
Monastery of San Lorenzo at Venice
Many lettered and traditional typographic ligatures derive from cursive handwriting, in which writers often connect characters without lifting pen from paper.
Special Collections, University of Iowa Libraries, Iowa City, Iowa.

Common typographic ligatures alleviate awkward areas where two letters overlap or create problematic spacing.

SO FRESH, SO DEF, SO STUPID

THE AARDVARK

Deconstructivist theorists

SUPER SCHOOL

If you find energy sticky

AMBIENT LAVA LAMP

Scruffy poetry sprees

THINK VANILLA

Affinity with happy gifts

Left:
Mrs. Eaves Ligatures
Typeface, 1996
Zuzana Licko
This text font is a revival not only of the work of John Baskerville but also of many ligatures previously lost to time. Over two hundred anachronistic and original ligatures add liveliness and eccentricity to the typeface.

ATypI
Logotype, 2005
Underware

So Fresh, So Def, So Stupid
Lettering, 2007
Justin Thomas Kay
A mountain of custom ligatures and letterforms turns otherwise ordinary type into memorable album cover lettering.

THE LIVES THEY LIVED

The Lives They Lived
Magazine cover, 2008
Typeface designed with
Patrick Griffin, Canada Type

**Why Art Is—and Is
Not—the New Fashion**
Customized editorial type,
2007

Angle of Repose
Lettering sketches and
magazine spread, 2008
*A font serves as the starting
point for lettering that complements the geometric lines of the
buildings shown in this article.*

Little Britain
Magazine spread, 2007

INTERVIEW: NANCY HARRIS ROUEMY

As a designer and art director at the New York Times Magazine, Nancy Harris Rouemy is responsible for many of the publication's memorable lettering and type treatments. Whether creating her own lettering or collaborating with a commissioned artist, Harris Rouemy complements the magazine's distinctive photography and illustration with equally compelling typography.

What are the reasons for customizing type in an editorial setting? Periodically, custom type is used to create a brand for a themed issue, as a means of signaling to the reader: "You are getting something special here; take notice and read!" Or it may be commissioned to push an idea when the photography needs a hand. If the photography is especially provocative, I want to marry the image with an arresting type solution—one in which content and form resonate.

Readers want to meet the face or place or thing that is described in the story, and there is no doubt that photographs establish an objective reality for the content. But every so often, type transmits a message that a photograph or classic illustration cannot. Lettering can convey layers of ideas that compel the reader to decode and interpret, and thus become more active in the viewing experience.

What are the editorial strengths and weaknesses of using lettering or type as a main visual element? As we become more and more entrenched in our computer era, lettering offers an infusion of freshness and surprise. There's a soulfulness, a humanistic quality that connects the reader to lettering. However, to affect the wow factor, specialized type solutions have to be used in a judicious manner. The pacing of a magazine is high priority; the balance between photography, illustration, the magazine's fonts and manip-ulated type treatments sustains visual pleasure. On occasion, it's just as important to exercise typographic restraint to allow the image to command the page.

How do you make the type and image relate to each other as well as the article? I always read the story first. The words and ideas revealed in the story will inspire the approach for the tone, the type, or a graphic element used for the design solution. Typographic pages facing photography or illustration must relate and play off of each other. Scale, structure, fonts, weights of letterforms, color, contrast, white space, alignments will constantly vary depending on the specific image at hand.

What is your creative relationship with letterers when you commission custom lettering as opposed to creating it yourself? I firmly believe that collaboration always produces the best results. Initially, I have a direction in mind. It's very much a back-and-forth developmental process, with both of us feeding off of each other's ideas.

What are the most important things to consider when creating custom letters? (1) Legibility and originality. (2) It's the deviated form that draws attention and produces something memorable.

LIFE BELOW

A CITY IS A LIVING THING... IT IS A BREATHING, PULSATING, MAN-MADE PHENOMENON WHOSE FOUNDATIONS GO DEEP INTO THE EARTH... THERE, IN THE WET CATACOMBS OF ITS ROOTS, TEEMS A LIFE QUITE UNKNOWN TO US IN THE FOREST OF TOWERS ABOVE..

BY Will Eisner

LETTERING AS IMAGE

THE OPAQUE WORD

Designers traditionally consider text and image as two separate compositional elements. Written content supplements or is supplemented by imagery, which may be photographic, informational, or illustrative. In some cases, however, letters themselves become the design's image and focal point.

The abstract nature of letterforms enables them to easily assume new visual personas—to adopt expressive, emotive, and informational qualities typically associated with images. When letters become imagery, they function on two levels: as a container for textual content and as an expression of a visual idea. Using lettering as image goes against book typography's precept that type should be an invisible crystal goblet. By making letters something to look at as well as to read, the designer asks the viewer to spend more time considering their forms and context, not just their content.

Artists have turned letterforms into imagery for thousands of years, distorting, warping, and reinventing the shapes of the alphabet to augment the underlying meaning and message of their words. Early Muslim artists avoided representational imagery, which they believed would lead to idolatry. Instead of the ubiquitous iconography of Christianity, Buddhism, and Hinduism, Islam communicates its faith through the abstract beauty of Arabic calligraphy. The supple strokes of the calligraphic alphabet reflect and glorify the text's transcendent message, not unlike the intricate letterforms found in medieval Bibles.

Such examples of decorative and illuminated lettering inspired nineteenth-century artists and designers to inject renewed levels of craft, detail, and ornament into lettering and type. Artists melded letterforms with plants, animals, and other physical objects, and illustrators wove alphabet letters and human figures into the same pictorial space. The Arts and Crafts movement renounced the mechanical commercialism of the Industrial Revolution for a more personal aesthetic of softer forms and handcrafted production methods. The small press movement's renewed emphasis on the hand of the artisan set the stage for the experimental lettering and organic modernism of Art Nouveau.

The artists of the Art Nouveau movement broke down distinctions between fine art, design, and craft. Architects, sculptors, and painters with and without formal lettering training turned to the alphabet as another avenue for their artistic creations.

The Spirit, "Life Below"
Illustration, 1948
Will Eisner
This comic book title page breaks the wall between text and image by integrating the main character's name into the illustration—the text becomes a staircase leading down into the gritty criminal underworld.
Courtesy of DC Comics and Denis Kitchen.

Ceramique Coilliot
Signage, 1898
Hector Guimard
This building and its ceramic sign, both designed by French architect Hector Guimard, express Art Nouveau's unified design approach through their shared organic forms.
Photo by Oliver Waine.

With fewer preconceived notions about the way letters should look, Art Nouveau artists broke free of traditional forms to create new and highly expressive alphabets that embody the movement's organic aesthetics. The letters in Art Nouveau signage and posters bend and curve with the elastic structure and flourishes of the plant world, also displaying an idiosyncratic touch of gothic lettering.

In the 1960s, San Francisco poster artists such as Rick Griffin and Victor Moscoso combined elements of Art Nouveau's flowing headlines with heavy ornamentation borrowed from nineteenth-century wood type to create a new language for letters. Just as the psychedelic music that their posters advertised was a reaction against social norms, these intensely human, acid-bent letterforms were a challenge to the era's prevailing cold modernism and orderly design. Letters curved, swelled, and squeezed across their designs, blurring the lines between text and image. Psychedelic experimentation meant not only to challenge the accepted forms of letters but also to inject new levels of meaning into words simply through their appearance.

Contemporary artists and designers have revived and reinterpreted the spirit and conceptual approach of psychedelic artists into a new psychedelia adapted to the digital age. Like its precursors, contemporary psychedelia can be viewed as a reactive movement—in this case a response to the speed, precision, and logic of digital technology. While many of these contemporary artists reject the computer in favor of obsessive hand-drawn lettering, some also exploit digital technology in an antithetical way to create dense, barely legible alphabets or compositions. Where the molten letterforms of the 1960s reflected a fun-seeking, free-flowing subculture, today's psychedelia commonly summons two opposite sides of the zeitgeist, evoking a paranoid and violent society or the overwhelming presence of commercial culture. Other contemporary letterers exploit digital tools to create highly rendered letters with a psychedelic disposition.

As letterforms transform into pattern or imagery, their text can become extremely difficult to decipher. Not everyone finds this problematic. What a designer loses in legibility might be recovered through the heightened graphic or narrative importance of the letters. Occasional trespasses across the boundaries of legibility or convention can sometimes enhance a visual or editorial statement. Letters that become imagery blur the lines between form and function as well as design and art.

Hand & Soul

Title page, 1896

William Morris

The classically inspired capitals of this Arts and Crafts title page cannot be separated from the organic patterning that envelops them.

Reproduced from Mosher Press Edition 1899. Image courtesy of Philip R. Bishop/Mosher Press website, hosted by Millersville University.

Quicksilver Messenger Service

Poster, 1968

Rick Griffin

Although many psychedelic poster artists pushed the extreme edges of legibility, their concert posters functioned as effective promotional tools by speaking the visual language of the 1960s counterculture.

Courtesy of the family of Rick Griffin.

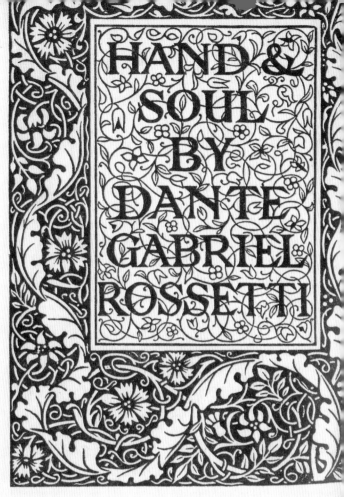

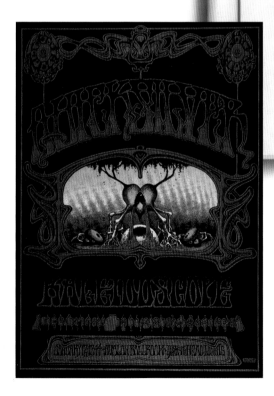

The Nassau Rake

Newspaper, 1852

Type foundries took advantage of wood type's freedom of scale to create elaborate, pictorial type designs. This detailed typeface (c. 1834) built entirely from caricatures is well suited to use as the masthead of a humorous college newspaper.

Organic
Lettering, 2007
Ryan Katrina with Mike
McQuade and Jamie Hall
These illustrative letters are
digitally collaged from photos
and drawings.

Blessphemy (of the
Peace Beast)
Album packaging, 2006
Seripop

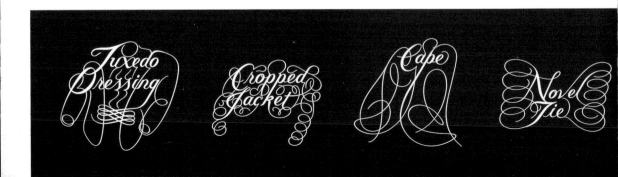

This page, top to bottom:

Architectural Alphabet
Alphabet, 2007
Abbott Miller
Many illustrative alphabets find the familiar forms of the roman alphabet in unexpected places. Miller's alphabet uses modern architectural floor plans to create a contemporary update of the neoclassical Architetonisches Alphabet (1773) by Johann David Steingruber.

Hypertype
Alphabet, 2005
Luke Ramsey and A. J. Purdy
Some illustrative alphabets are pure exercises in pictorial letterforms, the letters serving as a framework for artistic expression or commentary.

Want It!
Lettering, 2007
Marian Bantjes
Using an ornate script derived from the Saks Fifth Avenue logo, the words and extravagant flourishes in these whimsical lettering treatments suggest the clothing and accessories promoted by a Saks advertising campaign.

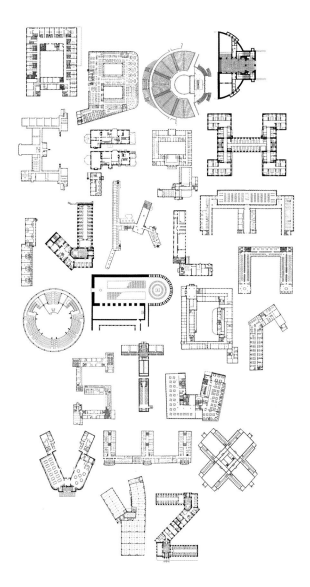

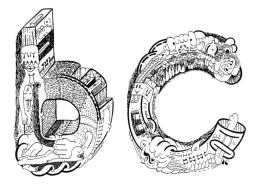

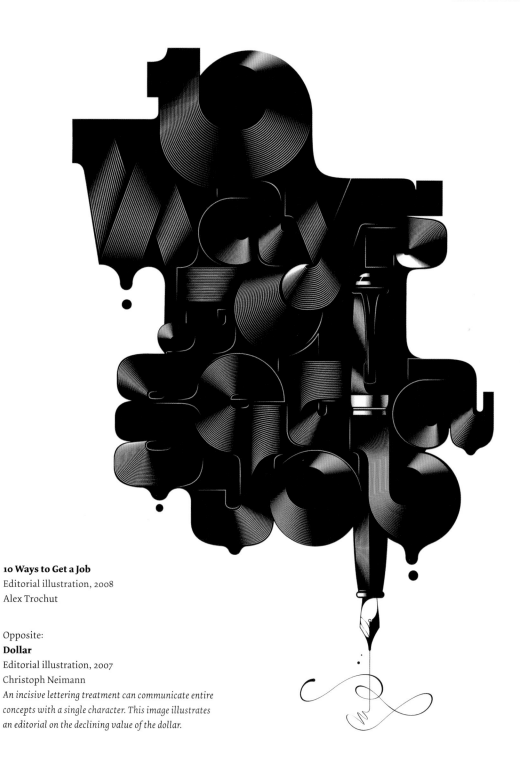

10 Ways to Get a Job
Editorial illustration, 2008
Alex Trochut

Opposite:
Dollar
Editorial illustration, 2007
Christoph Neimann
An incisive lettering treatment can communicate entire
concepts with a single character. This image illustrates
an editorial on the declining value of the dollar.

OOIOO
Screen-printed poster, 2007

Animal Collective
Photocopied flyer, 2004

Sightings
Photocopied flyer, 2005

Wzt Hearts
Color photocopied flyer, 2007

INTERVIEW: SHAUN FLYNN

The designs of musician and artist Shaun Flynn stand out on bulletin boards and record store shelves in his native Baltimore and around the country. Flynn's posters frequently incorporate elaborate or hidden lettering, in some cases abandoning any imagery in favor of a text-only solution.

You have a fine arts background. How did you get into lettering, which is often considered the realm of graphic design? I first began making posters out of necessity, for my bands in Baltimore. You've got a show, you need to promote it, and you want to make the poster look nice. Eventually other people began asking me to do flyers. I don't think I would have started making posters, especially for other people, without that aspect of self-promotion of the music I was playing.

What, if any, distinction do you see between making a text-based poster and creating a drawing or art installation? Both my posters and my artwork usually start with a simple material base and have a lo-fi, handmade process. With posters you have a single pen or a box of markers. I like taking a simple object or set of materials and turning it into something visually complex. I really appreciate bold simplicity, but I'm not a great "simple" designer. My work often winds up being ornate and taking a long time. It isn't necessarily ornate for its own sake but about whether or not I think it's worth putting the time into.

Why do you take a primarily hand-drawn approach to your flyers and posters? I never had a computer or took any computer courses in college. I really eschewed the graphic arts industry when I was in school. It wasn't something I considered having to use because, of course, I was going to be a "famous artist in New York." It became quickly apparent after I started making posters that the hand-drawn aspect was a big part of my interest. Handmade stuff is more interesting to me; your style emerges more quickly.

Your work often combines lettering and image into a single composition. Why do you approach posters in this unified way? I like integrating lettering into the imagery of the poster so that it really feels like one whole thing, not just some drawing from a sketchbook with words across the bottom. It makes an event seem more important when there's an image that can't be detached from the show. Sometimes I'll focus my energy on the information, the letters rather than the image—making the letters into the image themselves. It's pretty infinite what you can do to letters, and it's amazing what your brain will read. Anything can be very simply turned into some kind of letterform. There's really no reason or need to have anything else on a poster other than cool letters. If the poster is striking enough, whatever the degree of legibility, people will spend a little more time with it.

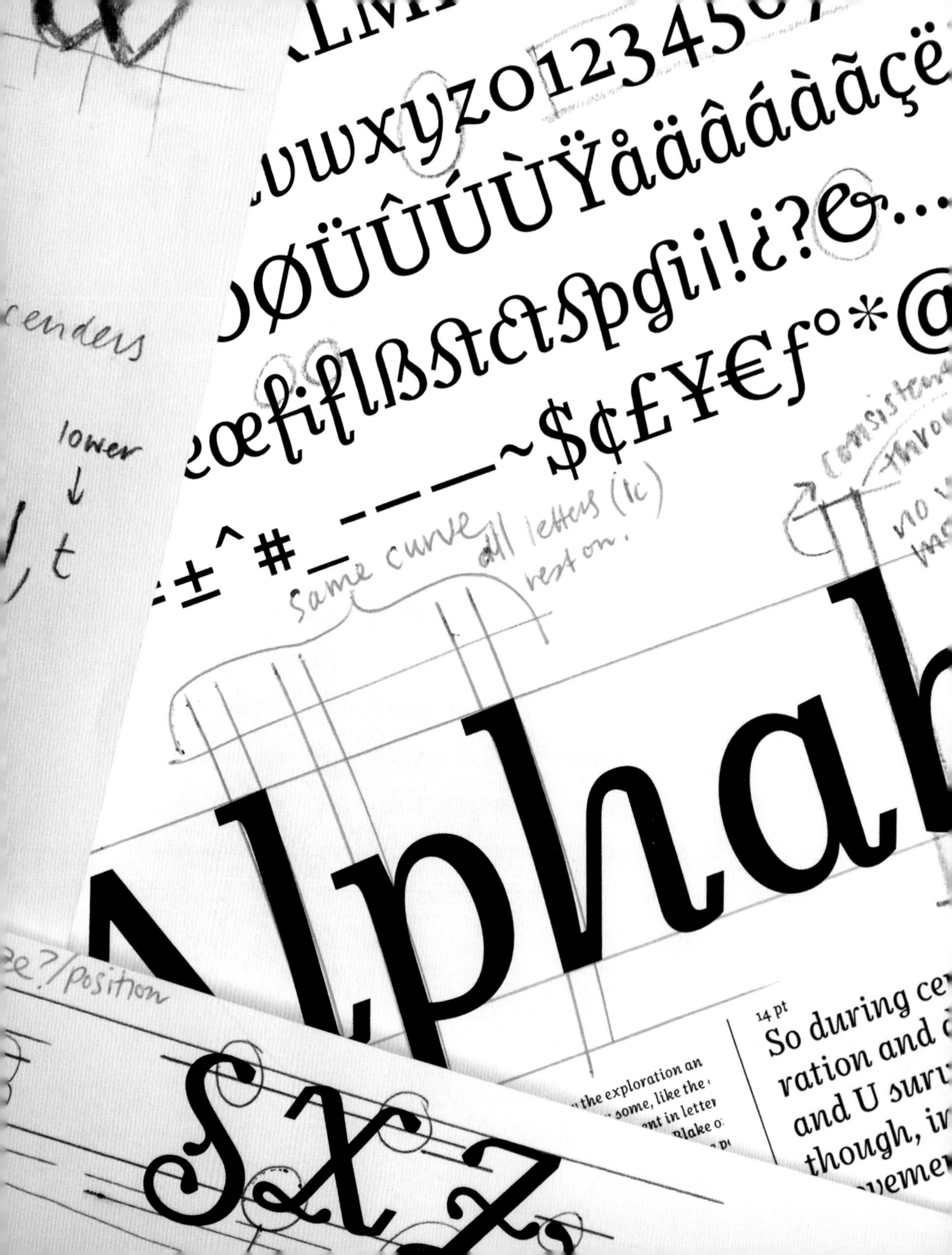

LMN

wxyzo1234567

ØÜÛÚÙŸÅäâáàãçë

œfiflßßtctspgfii!¿?&...

±^#_~$¢£¥€ƒº*@

same curve | all letters (lc) rest on.

no

consistent throughout

Alphab

So during ce
ration and
and U surv
though, in
vement

the exploration an
some, like the
nt in letter
Blake o

SxZ

DESIGNING TYPEFACES

BEHIND A FACE

Like any good design or lettering, a good typeface begins with an idea. Many times this is little more than a vague direction—making a "sexy looking" font or creating a typeface that's easy to read at small sizes. Other times a designer might have a more specific goal, such as wanting to fill a perceived stylistic void among available typefaces or developing a new interpretation of a classic face. Custom headlines, hand-painted signage, and other one-of-a-kind lettering inspire a number of typefaces attempting to reproduce the spirit of the original lettering, a much harder task than it appears. Lettering and type are two distinct practices, related in many ways, yet involving very different concerns and approaches. Where lettering produces a one-of-a-kind result that depends heavily on its context, type design emphasizes systems, consistency, and flexibility.

Any typeface, whether inspired by geometric principles or by the individuality of handwriting, differs from lettering in that all of its characters must work together equally well, no matter how they are arranged. Like a set of building blocks, a typeface is a kit of parts that can be reconfigured and reworked into countless forms on a moment's notice. The letters, figures, and symbols that compose this kit of parts should be a family of equals—individuals that are closely related and work hand in hand without one particular character calling attention to itself. Good typefaces function on the strength of their system and how the parts relate within the system. Great typefaces apply a beautiful and powerful system to articulate a strong idea.

Along with a concept, a thorough grasp of a typeface's intended use helps a designer navigate the thousands or even millions of major and minor decisions that shape the face. A designer working on a book face will make choices favoring legibility at text sizes over those favoring the font's large-scale appearance. Conversely, display fonts may emphasize subtle detailing and construction that enhance use at large point sizes. A typeface created as a companion to an existing font should echo some of its partner's attributes. While a type designer can never predict every possible use of a font, a typeface created without any application in mind may be self-fulfillingly useless. Those who know how to *use* type as well as design it have a greater understanding of a font's design requirements—it is no accident that many early printers also created their own type.

Sketches for Odile
Type sketches and proofs,
2000–2005
Sibylle Hagmann, Kontour
*Common steps in the type
design process include sketches
and many rounds of printed
and marked-up proofs. For
the design of Odile, Hagmann
reinterpreted the characteristics
of Charter, an unfinished
1936 display face by William
Addison Dwiggins, into a
contemporary book type family.*

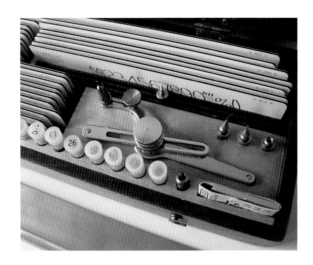

Conflict
Zen Arcade
PROFANE EXISTENCE
amphetamine

Dig if you will the picture of *you and I*
Invisible man who can sing in a visible voice
Hours slipping by as you watch the worlds collide

Below:

Twin
Typeface system and web application, 2003
Letterror

Twin resulted from a type design competition for the cities of Minneapolis and St. Paul, Minnesota. Rather than represent the cities with a single typeface, Letterror created a system of fonts, ranging from no-nonsense sans serifs and casual scripts to unconventional, decorative letters. To deploy its palette of ten type styles, Letterror developed a web application to automatically change the fonts and appearance of text based on user input and outside data, such as current temperature and weather conditions in the Twin Cities.

Above:

Bryant
Typeface, 2002–2005
Eric Olson, Process Type Foundry

Before the advent of transfer lettering and digital type, drafters sometimes employed mechanical lettering kits to rapidly draw professional-looking letters. Bryant reinvents these no-frills alphabets as a sophisticated digital typeface, adding typographic refinements like tapers, stroke modulation, and a family of bold, italic, and condensed weights.

3 Twin CITIES DESIGN Celebration 2003 T>cities>DESIGN>CELEBRATION>2003 Twin Cities
BRATION 2003 t cities design celebration 2003 Twin_c_d_Celebration_03 TWIN+Cities+d+c
s_d_CELEBRATION_II003 Twin cities D C 03 TWIN_CITIES_D_C_200III t Cities design CELEB
bration_03 +:CITIES:design:Celebra+ion:II003 Twin c design c 2003 twin Cities DESIGN c 03
GN celebration 03 t c D Celebration 03 Twin C DESIGN celebration 03 twin cities design CEL
bration 03 t Cities DESIGN Celebration 200III t C design CELEBRATION 2003 twin CITIES d
bration 2003 twin D 2003 c DESIGN Celebration T Cities D CELEBRATION
>Cities>Design>Celebration>2003 Twin>C>Design>CELEBRATION>2003 T c:i:E:S DESIGN C
2003 T Design C 03 Twin c d c 2003 t cities D C 2003 Twin>c>design>c> Twin/C/I
2003 t c d celebration oIII t CITIES design C 03 twin C design Celebtation 200III t:c:D:CELE
ties/Design/C/03 t+Cities+DESIGN+c+2003 twin/Cities/Design/c/2003 twin CITIES d cele
TION+II003 T cities d c 03 TWIN+c+D+CELEBRATION+2003 +W:n+c+Design+CELEBRATION+20
N c:i:E:S design c 2003 t c design c 03 TWIN cities CELEBRATION 2003 T cities design c
Design+c+03 Twin/Cities/DESIGN/celebration/2003 TWIN C Design Celebration 03 TWIN

nmrhpbklijf

CHARACTER TRAITS

Forms and motifs repeat throughout a typeface's system. Although small variations occur from letter to letter, type designers employ a common palette of shapes from which to consistently approach the construction of new characters.

Type designers do not read the alphabet from A through Z. Instead, they separate and categorize letters according to their individual traits. The diagonally shaped letter A stands closer to W than to B, while the d might follow the p in sequence of design. By analyzing and grouping characters that share traits, a type designer can better refine and standardize the typeface's system. Breaking the letters down to their separate elements and characteristics enables a designer to treat letters consistently throughout a font. The design requirements of a capital R can be understood by analyzing the characteristics of the P and K.

Most type designers begin drawing with n and o for the lowercase characters and H and O for the uppercase. These control characters are examples of square and round letters, and resolving their stroke weight, width, x-height, axis, and other physical characteristics starts the process of fleshing out and refining the font's system. Once a designer is happy with the first two characters, and their relationship to each other, he or she will try drawing a few other letters. These are usually characters that share some traits with the control characters but present new design challenges, such as the lowercase p and h or capital R and U. Making the correct decisions and fixing any issues at this early stage of the process are crucial, as any problems or mistakes are amplified through the rest of the character set. A problematic p or h may signal flaws in the o or n. It is easier to change the serifs or stroke thickness on a handful of letters than to go back and revise the entire font. After the first four or five letters are resolved, a type designer usually considers at least one diagonal character such as the v or A, and other potentially challenging letters like the a or B.

ROGUES GALLERY
Otherwise well-made lettering falls apart when the characters are used out of their original context. Type must adapt to infinite groupings of words, while custom lettering needs to fulfill only the requirements of its particular application.

Since letters in a typeface rarely stand alone, combining the letters into words and sequences is a critical test that begins as early in the process as possible. If two of the characters do not look good next to each other, one, both, or even the entire system must be adjusted to make them work. Only after refining these first half dozen or so letters does a designer move on to the rest of the character set. By fine-tuning and figuring out how to combine the various traits—square, round, diagonal—a type designer creates a roadmap for building the rest of the typeface.

Abrupt Ado
brupt Ado
HOTEL ODEO
HOTEL ODEON
Open Diner
Open Diner
Metal Elegar
Metal Elegar

Odile and Elido
Typefaces, 2006 and 2008
Sibylle Hagmann, Kontour
*While many of the same rules apply
to both serif and sans serif typefaces,
serif characters have their own sets
of concerns. Merely attaching serifs
to an existing sans does not make
a serif face. Adjustments for stroke
weight, color, and spacing must
all be considered when applying
these rules to a serif font. Serif
faces generally have greater stroke
contrast and letterspacing.*

Photo by Isaac Gertman.

Gotham
Typeface, 2000
Tobias Frere-Jones, H&FJ
*The inspiration for Gotham
consisted mainly of capital
letters found on metal
and hand-painted signage
in New York. Frere-Jones
began the typeface by
drawing the capitals and
then matched them with
a compatible lowercase
alphabet.*

LETTERFORM ANALYSIS

The diagrams on the following pages illustrate some basic principles, nuances, and considerations for constructing each letter of the alphabet, loosely grouped by their shared forms. Even this stripped-down, sans serif font (Franklin Gothic) contains many subtleties of design and demonstrates centuries-old conventions. Because of space limitations, *Lettering & Type* can diagram only this transitional sans serif typeface, but applying these same critiques and observations elsewhere forms a basis for understanding the principles and idiosyncrasies of any typeface's system. Letters do not occur in isolation; designers and letterers have compared and learned from precedent for thousands of years. Digital technology's ability to overlap and scale type makes comparing two letters or fonts easier than ever. A type designer can quickly analyze and contrast the traits of several existing typefaces, making it easy to see what works and what doesn't.

LOWERCASE

Type designers typically draw at least some of the lower- and uppercase characters concurrently to get a sense of the relationships between the two cases. Which case is prioritized or resolved first depends on the end use as well as the originating idea. Text typefaces emphasize the lowercase, since these characters will find the most use. While a book font can get by with a workmanlike uppercase, the lowercase characters often make or break a typeface. Decisions about the x-height, length of ascenders and descenders, serif size, character width, counter space, crossbar placement, and curve shape dramatically affect a font's overall feel, legibility, and usefulness. Since the lowercase does not take kindly to increased letterspacing, establishing accurate spacing and side bearings for the lowercase alphabet is extremely important.

Although the conventions illustrated on these pages apply to most fonts, not every typeface adheres to these practices—some purposely ignore them or even invent their own rules. Each font's individual system provides its own formula and rationale for how and when these guidelines are followed.

Visit Underware's TypeWorkshop.com for more type design and lettering basics. For additional letter-by-letter diagrams and comparisons of both serif and san serif fonts, see Karen Cheng's Designing Type *(New Haven, CT: Yale University Press, 2005).*

Many designers begin a typeface by drawing the lowercase n. Once the n is perfected, the u, h, and m quickly follow suit. While all four letters are similar, they usually have subtle variations in emphasis, curvature, and width.

The shoulders of the n, m, and h push to the upper right, balancing the weight of the stems and emphasizing the forward motion of reading and writing.

The rounded portions of the letters overshoot the x-height or baseline.

Considerable tapering at the join keeps this area of the letter from appearing too dark.

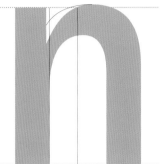

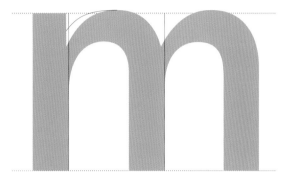

The m's counters are approximately the same shape and area as the counter of the n. In some typefaces the m's counters are slightly narrower.

The two counter spaces of the m are optically equal in area.

ınnnnnnmmmmmmmuuuuuuuuhhhhhh.

The counters of the n, m, u, and h are not symmetrical.

The finish and appearance of the stems' tips—flat, angled, serifed, flared, or other—are reflected throughout the font's system.

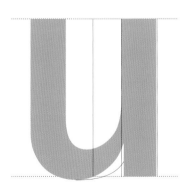

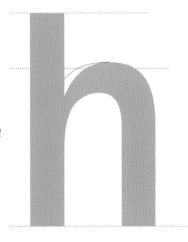

In fonts with greater stroke contrast, the right stem of the u is typically thinner than the left. In Franklin Gothic there is only a slight difference.

The length and appearance of the ascenders establish important relationships between the x-height, cap height, and ascender height.

To avoid appearing small next to square and diagonal characters, the round lowercase letters all have overshoots and slightly broader widths.

The lowercase o maintains more circular proportions in some typefaces, especially in geometric sans serifs and modern faces. Less common is a boxy and flat-sided o, which can reduce or even eliminate the need for overshoots.

The stroke emphasis of the o also determines the typeface's axis. Franklin Gothic has a vertical axis. Humanist typefaces typically have oblique stress, and the axis may vary from character to character.

The overhang of the c does not extend beyond the lower stroke.

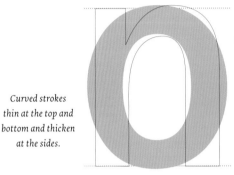

Curved strokes thin at the top and bottom and thicken at the sides.

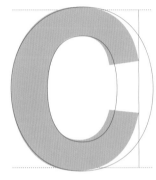

A c with an aperture that is too large may exhibit uneven color; however, apertures that are too small reduce legibility.

The shape of the counter and outside curves of the o establish the rounded forms that are carried throughout the typeface's system.

The c is narrower than the o to compensate for its added negative space.

o o o o o o o o c c c c c c c e e e e e e e a a a a a a a a

Significant thinning of both round and horizontal strokes keeps the e from filling in and appearing too dark.

The top of the a is slightly narrower than its bowl, to keep the letter from seeming top-heavy and unbalanced.

In some fonts, the a incorporates a short tail or a transitive serif that references the exit mark of the pen.

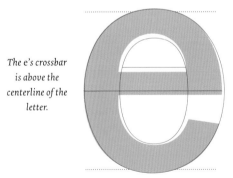

The e's crossbar is above the centerline of the letter.

Significant thinning and tapering of the horizontals prevent the two-story a from appearing too dark and congested.

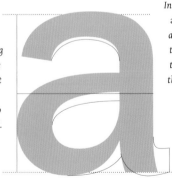

In old style and transitional fonts, the eye of the e is typically asymmetrical and sometimes enclosed with a diagonal crossbar.

Like many twentieth-century sans serifs, Franklin Gothic's two-story a possesses a large bowl and narrow aperture. The a in humanist fonts typically has a much shorter bowl.

The single-story version of the a, frequently found in italics and geometric sans serifs, is similar in construction to the q.

Because of their angled strokes and joins, diagonal characters typically display increased stroke contrast and tapering.

The v's left diagonal is thicker than its right. This difference in stroke weight is more pronounced in faces with high contrast.

The w is narrower than the m and is frequently asymmetrical.

Thinning and tapering, especially noticeable on the middle strokes, maintain the w's even color.

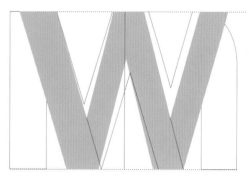

The strokes of many vs taper as they approach the join. Ink traps exist at the joins in some bolder typefaces.

The angles of the w's two middle strokes differ from those of the outer strokes, to keep the character from becoming too wide.

On some bold fonts, ink traps may be added to relieve heaviness at the joins.

VVVVVVVWWW**WWW**WWWXXXX**X**XXXXyy**y**y**y**yyy

The lowercase x gives the illusion of being a symmetrical character.

The strokes of the y taper into the join.

The top half of the x is slightly shorter and narrower than the bottom half, to avoid top-heaviness.

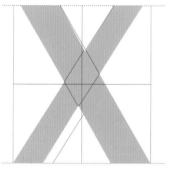

The slightly thicker left diagonal reflects the font's stroke emphasis.

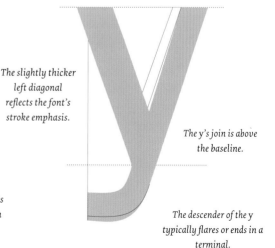

The y's join is above the baseline.

Subtle, or occasionally prominent, offsets and stroke tapering maintain the x's optical balance.

Stroke weight and emphasis follow the axis and pattern of the typeface's system.

The descender of the y typically flares or ends in a terminal.

The base of the k's leg extends beyond its upper arm, to keep the letter from appearing top-heavy.

The z's diagonal breaks the rules of stroke emphasis and axis; in weight it is similar to strokes that follow the opposite axis, top left to bottom right. This anomaly reflects a change in the angle of translation. Without this emphasis, the z would appear too light, especially in serif fonts.

The z is usually narrower than the n.

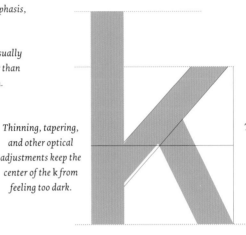

Thinning, tapering, and other optical adjustments keep the center of the k from feeling too dark.

The diagonal stroke may taper slightly.

The waist of the k is above its centerline.

The bottom of the z is wider than its top.

The k's three counter spaces enclose relatively equal areas of negative space.

zzzzzzzzkkkkkk

ROGUES GALLERY

n

This n is too wide, and its curved top lacks an overshoot.

h

The counter of the h is symmetrical, making the letter's shoulder slump backward.

m

This m's right counter is too narrow.

c

This c's aperture and top stroke are both too wide.

e

A low, heavy crossbar and short finial make this e top-heavy and out of proportion.

a

This a has insufficient stroke thinning, and its top curve extends beyond the letter's bowl.

v

This v appears wide, and lack of stroke tapering makes its join too dark.

x

This perfectly symmetrical x lacks tapers and appears top-heavy.

y

The strokes of this y join at the baseline, making its counter too large and its tail too short.

Like the n, m, u, *and* h, *the letters* p, q, b, *and* d *are all similar in
design. However, they are not merely the same letter flipped or rotated—
separate adjustments in emphasis and axis occur for each letter.*

*Thinning and tapering at the joins prevent these
areas of the letter from becoming too heavy.*

*The p, q, b, and d are narrower than the o, and
their counters are slightly more condensed.*

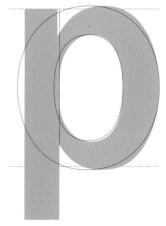

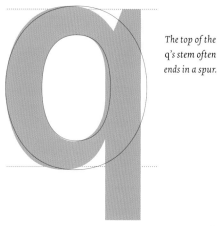

*The top of the
q's stem often
ends in a spur.*

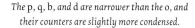

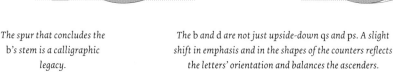

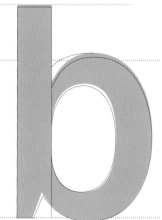

*Tapering
maintains even
color at small
sizes.*

*The spur that concludes the
b's stem is a calligraphic
legacy.*

*The b and d are not just upside-down qs and ps. A slight
shift in emphasis and in the shapes of the counters reflects
the letters' orientation and balances the ascenders.*

The balance of proportions among its three counter spaces defines the g's appearance. Even though their shapes differ, the color and enclosed areas of the two bowls roughly correspond.

The curves and angles of the lowercase s relate to (without necessarily duplicating) the slightly more condensed forms of the capital S.

Like the strokes of the e and the a, those of the two-story g are thinned to maintain even color.

The top bowl of the g is more rounded and narrower than its lower loop.

Thinning of the top and bottom horizontals keeps the s from appearing too dark.

The s is not two joined semicircles. The distinct curves of the bowls join through the s's straight spine.

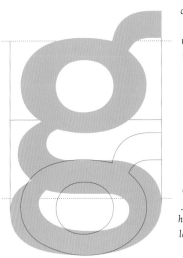

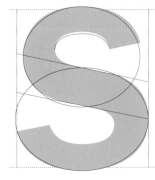

The single-story version of the g, more common in italics and modernist sans serifs, is easier to construct than its two-story sibling. One-story gs usually share traits with the bowl of the q.

Fonts with long descenders frequently have gs with larger loops.

The bottom bowl of the s is wider and taller than the top bowl.

gggggggggssssss

ROGUES GALLERY

Z

This z lacks an adjusted stroke axis, and its base is too narrow.

k

The unbalanced counters and high join of this k create an awkward figure.

p

Lack of an overshoot makes this p's bowl feel too small.

b

This b's bowl is the same size as the o's, and it lacks tapers at its joins.

g

The bowls of this g are too similar in shape and lack sufficient stroke thinning.

j

This j's dot is too small and high, while its wide tail causes spacing problems.

r

This r is too wide, and its join is too high, causing the letter to space and color unevenly.

t

A symmetrical crossbar and extended tail make this t appear to tilt backward.

f

This f's crossbar extends too far leftward, while the terminal is too far right.

Many designers further differentiate the l by extending its ascender above the cap height or by adding a humanist angle to its peak.

A slightly thinner stroke weight differentiates Franklin Gothic's lowercase l from its capital I.

The dots of typefaces with large x-heights, like Franklin Gothic, are generally closer to the i's stem. Faces with short x-heights benefit from more generous space around the dot.

The narrow widths of the f, t, and r help reduce these asymmetrical characters' spacing problems.

Rounded dots usually overshoot the stem width to compensate for the softness of their circular form.

The j's curved descender distinguishes it from the similar i.

Serifed ls mimic the design of the h's stem.

The i's stem is a shortened version of the l.

Type designers take many different approaches to the j's tail—various terminals, angles, curves, and lengths are common.

The tail of the j is often (although not always) similar to the y's descender.

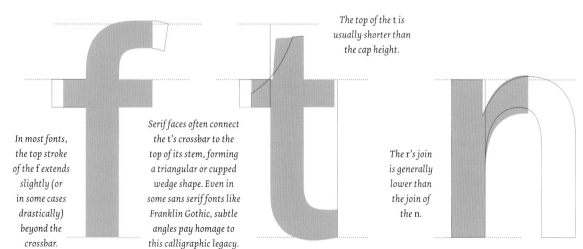

The top of the t is usually shorter than the cap height.

In most fonts, the top stroke of the f extends slightly (or in some cases drastically) beyond the crossbar.

Serif faces often connect the t's crossbar to the top of its stem, forming a triangular or cupped wedge shape. Even in some sans serif fonts like Franklin Gothic, subtle angles pay homage to this calligraphic legacy.

The r's join is generally lower than the join of the n.

The tail of the t is slightly longer than its crossbar.

The crossbars of the f and t are disproportionately to the right of the stem, to balance the letters' negative space and emphasize their forward motion. This asymmetry is even more pronounced in serif typefaces.

In lieu of a terminal, the r's stroke flares out to add mass to the right side of the letter. In serif faces, terminals are usually held close to the stem or tucked below the stroke to reduce the character's awkward negative space.

The H is narrower than the round O.

The H is a control character for the uppercase, and its attributes set the standard for all of the square capitals.

The E is narrower than the H, compensating for its open right side.

The center arm of the E is noticeably shorter and somewhat thinner than the top and bottom arms.

The H's crossbar in most typefaces is placed slightly higher than half of the cap height.

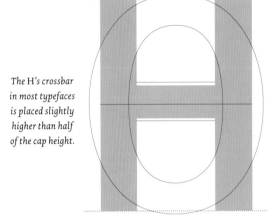

Like the crossbar of the H, the E's middle arm is slightly above the center line.

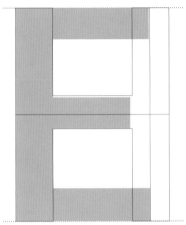

Horizontal strokes are thinner than verticals. Even in typefaces with no apparent contrast, a slight emphasis on the verticals is necessary to counter the illusion that horizontal strokes are thicker than stems.

The bottom arm of the E usually extends beyond the top two arms.

HHHHHHHHHEEEEEEEE

UPPERCASE

Maintaining the relationship of proportions between uppercase and lowercase usually means that a font's capitals, customarily taller than the lowercase, are also wider and occupy more space than their shorter counterparts. To compensate for this additional area and white space, the stroke weight of most capital letters is slightly heavier than that of the lowercase. Uppercase characters with the same stroke thickness as their lowercase counterparts often feel light by comparison. Type designers typically condense the uppercase characters slightly, to prevent the capitals from dominating the smaller lowercase alphabet and to maintain more consistent widths throughout the font. The lowercase ascenders do not necessarily define the cap height—the uppercase of many fonts is shorter than the height of the ascenders.

A narrow width and slightly heavier stroke weight help offset the F's irregular shape.

Serif typefaces often reduce the awkward spacing of the E, F, T, and L with enlarged and heavy serifs that fill some of the space within each character.

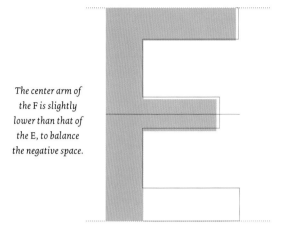

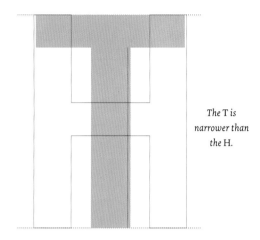

The center arm of the F is slightly lower than that of the E, to balance the negative space.

The T is narrower than the H.

The stroke weight of the stem is increased to balance the T's overall lightness.

FFFFFFFTTTTTTTTLLLLLLLLIIIIIIIIII

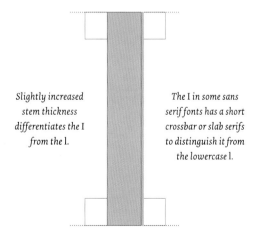

A thicker stroke weight compensates for the L's light color.

Slightly increased stem thickness differentiates the I from the l.

The I in some sans serif fonts has a short crossbar or slab serifs to distinguish it from the lowercase l.

The L is a problematic character for type designers because of its large, asymmetrical open space. Making the L significantly narrower improves (but does not eliminate) spacing issues.

In serif fonts the I's serifs mimic the top of the L and bottom of the T.

O is the second uppercase control character. The curvature and width of the O influence the design of other round capitals.

Like other rounded characters, the O, C, Q, and G overshoot the cap height and baseline.

The overhang or terminal of the C does not extend beyond the lower stroke.

As a rounded character, the O is wider than the H, especially in faces with a circular, geometric O.

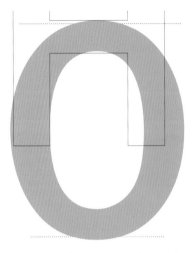

The counter shape and the axis of stroke emphasis of the O, like those of the o, are critical manifestations of the typeface's system.

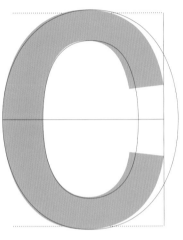

The O possesses a rounded, modulated stroke. At its heaviest, the O's stroke is wider than the stem of the H, while at its narrowest, the stroke is thinner than the H's crossbar.

Like its lowercase counterpart, the C is narrower than the O.

OOOOOOOCCCCCCCQQQQQQQGGGGGG

Some Gs replace the crossbar with short serifs or even do without any horizontal element.

The G is wider than the C.

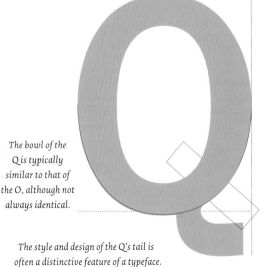

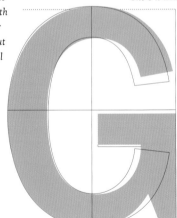

The crossbar or serif height falls below the letter's centerline.

The bowl of the Q is typically similar to that of the O, although not always identical.

The style and design of the Q's tail is often a distinctive feature of a typeface. Designers approach the tail in a variety of ways, especially in serif fonts. Unlike Franklin Gothic, many other transitional sans serifs have a straight stroke that extends into the bowl.

To maintain legibility and color, the G's crossbar is thinned and does not extend past the middle of the letter.

Some Gs have a spur at their lower right corner.

Although D and O are similar, the D's curve and counter shape differ from those of the O.

Stroke thinning keeps the B's interior from becoming too dark.

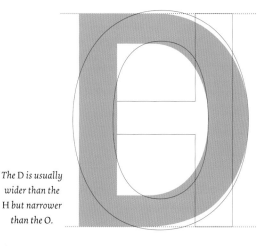

The curved strokes taper at the B's waist, where they meet above the centerline.

The D is usually wider than the H but narrower than the O.

The lower bowl of the B is slightly wider and taller than the top bowl, placing the letter's crossbar above the centerline.

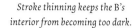

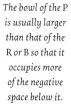

The bowl of the P is usually larger than that of the R or B so that it occupies more of the negative space below it.

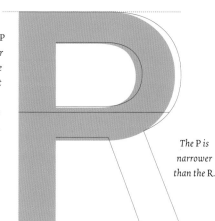

The R's bowl occupies slightly more than half of the cap height.

The P is narrower than the R.

The crossbar of the R thins to maintain even color.

On some old style and transitional typefaces, the bottom of the P's bowl does not connect to the stem.

The R's leg tapers into the bowl. The location of this join varies from font to font, but it is rarely at the intersection of the stem.

In most fonts, the R's leg extends past the letter's bowl. Franklin Gothic's compact R is an exception to this custom.

The right diagonal is slightly thicker than the left diagonal. This difference is more pronounced in typefaces with greater contrast.

The V is slightly narrower than the A.

The amount of negative space within the A is balanced between the two counters to keep the upper counter from becoming tight and pinched.

A thinned crossbar and strokes that taper toward the apex maintain the upper counter's open space.

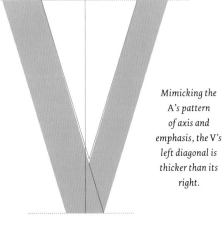

Mimicking the A's pattern of axis and emphasis, the V's left diagonal is thicker than its right.

The crossbar of a typical A falls well below the centerline.

The A's outer angles are similar, to maintain a sense of symmetry and to approximate the angles of the V.

The V's strokes taper as they approach the join. Bolder weights often employ ink traps where the strokes meet.

AAAAAAAAVVVVVVVVXXXXXXXXWWWWWW

Although this is rarely the case, the X gives the impression of two diagonal strokes crossing in the center.

Unlike the lowercase w and m, the capital W is often wider than the M.

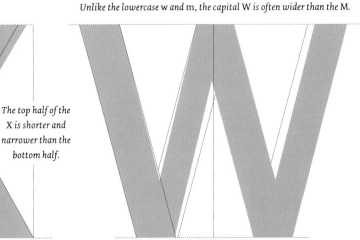

The top half of the X is shorter and narrower than the bottom half.

To maintain the illusion of symmetry, type designers offset the X's strokes.

As stroke contrast between the two diagonals increases, greater offsetting is necessary.

Stroke tapering keeps the center of the character from becoming too heavy.

Prominent thinning and tapering, especially on the inner strokes, keep the W's color consistent.

The two inner diagonals may be drawn at different angles from the outer strokes.

Some designers add ink traps to relieve heaviness at the W's joins.

The K's three counter spaces are made relatively equal in area, to maintain visual balance.

Like other diagonal characters, the Y has a left diagonal that is slightly heavier than its right one, maintaining proper stroke emphasis.

Significant thinning and a subtle ink trap reduce the darkness where the diagonal joins the stem.

The K's diagonal strokes meet above the centerline.

The two diagonals taper into the join.

The Y's stem is shorter than the diagonal strokes.

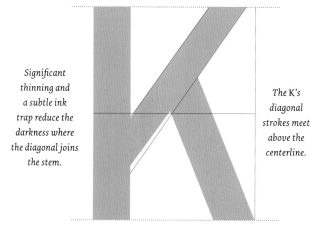

The leg of the K extends farther than its arm and is noticeably heavier.

KKKKKKKYYYYYYYY

ROGUES GALLERY

H

This wide H has a too-heavy crossbar.

E

This symmetrical E has arms of equal length, making it look awkward.

F

The lower arm of the F is too high and wide.

T

This T's stem is light, and its crossbar is too wide.

L

This L's broadness accentuates its uneven negative space.

G

This G's crossbar is wide and placed too high; its top curve extends past its base.

C

This C is too wide, and the top stroke hangs beyond its base.

B

This symmetrical B has bowls of equal size, giving it a top-heavy look.

P

This P's bowl is too high and pinched.

R

The long leg and small bowl of this R distribute the negative space unevenly while darkening the join.

Because of their diagonal strokes and thick joins, the N and M present challenges to creating characters of a consistent stroke weight.

The M's diagonals meet at a similar angle to those of the V, but with subtle attenuation of the strokes.

Type designers frequently introduce ink traps to reduce heaviness at the joins of the N and M.

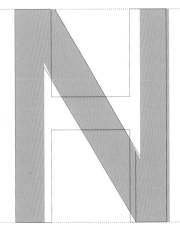

The N's diagonal stroke is heavier than its thinned verticals.

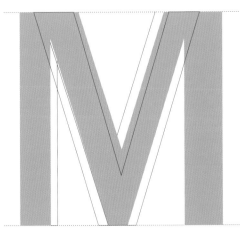

The stems of the N and M are often narrower than their apices, to allow increased negative space within these letters.

Like the N's stems, those of the M are significantly thinned—in some fonts the stems also taper into the joins.

The vertex of the M is narrow, and even pointed in some typefaces.

NNNNNNNNNMMMMMMMMMZZZZZZ

ROGUES GALLERY

Diagonals of equal length and lack of tapering make this K dark and top-heavy.

Overextended serifs cause spacing problems.

Inverted emphasis makes this A appear backward, while a too-high crossbar pinches its upper counter.

The Z's top is narrower than its base.

This Y's stem is too tall, and its stroke emphasis is backward.

Four similar diagonals increase the W's width and create dark areas at the joins.

Like the lowercase z's diagonal, the capital Z's does not conform to the rules of stroke emphasis and axis visible in other diagonal characters. The Z's diagonal is similar in stroke weight to the right diagonal of the A, referencing a change in axis of the broad-nibbed pen. This adjustment maintains the Z's color.

In typefaces with high stroke contrast, the right stem of the U is thinner than the left. In Franklin Gothic there is only moderate differentiation.

The J is one of the narrowest capital letters. As its tail gets wider and more hooked, the J's left side become less balanced and more difficult to space.

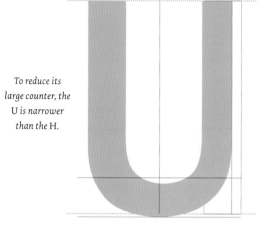

To reduce its large counter, the U is narrower than the H.

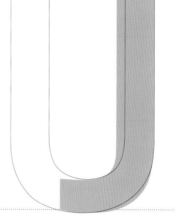

The lowercase j and y and the capital S's lower bowl provide models for the J's tail.

Like other characters, the U's stroke weight lightens in the horizontal portions of the stroke.

On serif faces, the tail often ends with a terminal or flare.

The tails of humanist Js sometimes descend below the baseline.

UUUŬUUUJJJJJJJJSSS**SS**SSS

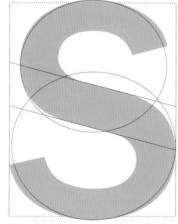

The design of the uppercase S is similar to that of the lowercase.

Stroke thinning is applied to the top and bottom bowls but less drastically than on the lowercase form.

ROGUES GALLERY

N

Lack of thinning and of ink traps causes the N to become too dark.

Z

This Z lacks an adjusted stroke axis, and its base is too narrow.

U

Reversed stroke emphasis on this too-wide U makes it seem backward.

J

This J's wide hook creates spacing problems.

S

This symmetrical S with a horizontal spine appears top-heavy and disjointed.

Like its lowercase counterpart, the S is not two joined semicircles. Its straight spine connects the distinct curves of the two bowls.

The bottom bowl of the S is wider and taller than the top bowl, preserving the letter's stability.

a) 928 457 610

b) 633 902 174

c) 187 629 055

TABULAR, LINING FIGURES

My 807 gerbils

$24,736,901.85

1 mile, 3 lights

TEXT (OLD STYLE) FIGURES

When numbers appear in body copy, text figures like 90,825 are used to match the proportions and rhythm of the lowercase alphabet.

NUMERALS

Like their architectural counterpart, a building's street number, the numerals of more than a few typefaces are underdeveloped afterthoughts. However, numerals can strongly shape a font's personality or make an otherwise reserved typeface distinctive. A well-designed set of numerals can be justification enough for a typographer to employ a font. Unlike letters, which must combine as words to have meaning, numbers have concrete definitions and significance on their own. A type designer can safely assume that a g will rarely be used outside the context of other letters, yet it is not uncommon to see a 6, 1, or 5 working solo as a page number, price tag, or street sign. Type designers must consider this expanded end use when developing numerals for their typefaces.

Early fonts included only a single set of text figures or "old style" numerals of varying heights and baselines. These deviating heights correspond to the lowercase characters' ascenders, descenders, and calligraphic origins and are meant for use among text. Accompanying the proliferation of commercial typography in the eighteenth century, numbers began to play a more prominent role in the printed world, appearing in numerical tables, charts, dates, and lists. Reflecting these new uses, type foundries introduced alternate styles of numerals to their fonts. Lining numerals sit on the baseline and all have the same height, often equivalent to the cap height or slightly shorter. Tabular figures have equal widths and spacing to create well-aligned and uniform tables, columns, and charts. These two developments proved so useful and popular that by the twentieth century many fonts were released with only a single set of lining, tabular numbers, at the expense of the traditional, text-friendly old style figures.

While lining and tabular figures are perfect for mathematical and numerical applications, they tend to look out of place when used among lowercase text. Contemporary type designers have revived the practice of releasing multiple sets of numerals with their typefaces, to address the widest possible variety of applications. Like any other aspect of a typeface, end use should guide design of numbers—text figures are the natural and useful numeral style for a book typeface, while a display family usually features lining numerals.

!!!
Album artwork, 2004
Ray Hearn, Shinya Horiuchi
Original !!! logo by
Daniel Gorman

å RING

à GRAVE

ç CEDILLA

é ACUTE

î CIRCUMFLEX

ñ TILDE

ö UMLAUT OR
DIAERESIS

š CARON

*A basic set of accent marks is
required for English and most
European languages. Additional
accents and phonetic characters
can adapt the roman alphabet
to even more languages.*

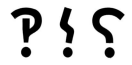

*Over the years, various writers,
linguists, and typographers
have introduced and attempted
to popularize new punctuation
marks. These three proposed
symbols—the interrobang (a
combination of ? and !), the
irony mark, and the rhetorical
question mark—have not found
widespread recognition or use.*

PUNCTUATION AND ACCENTS

Punctuation organizes, clarifies, and modifies written language. It does? Absolutely! Letters may form the core of a font, but the secondary characters—punctuation marks, symbols, and accented characters—play an important and sometimes overlooked role in typography. A font's punctuation and diacritics should quickly and clearly communicate their intended meaning or modification. Poorly sized, spaced, or drawn punctuation marks and accents look out of place within their font and can even corrupt a word's meaning or pronunciation. Well-designed symbols effectively convey their modifications and meaning without breaking the flow of text, working purposefully yet comfortably among the alphabet letters. Type designers treat punctuation and symbols with the same care as any other character, unifying the traits of each secondary mark with the typeface's overall system.

A Plastic-Tipped Cigar

A Plastic-Tipped Cigar

A Plastic-Tipped Cigar

A Plastic-Tipped Cigar

Auto
Type family, 2004
Underware

The slope angle of italics can vary: anything between three and twenty degrees is fair game, while ten to fourteen degrees is average. The Auto family contains three different italics, set apart by each font's unique style, angle, and level of calligraphic influence. All three accomplish the italic's primary job of standing out amid roman characters.

TYPE FAMILIES

Much like running a small business, typography can be made easier (and sometimes messier) by getting the family involved. The power to harness multiple weights and styles of a typeface gives typographers an arsenal of tools and extra choices if a particular font weight refuses to work. While many display typefaces, especially the more unusual or ornamental varieties, may consist of a single font, typical uses demand that text faces include at least three or four styles: regular (roman), italic (oblique), bold (demi), and small caps.

Crushin'

Crushin'

Crushin'

Crushin'

Crushin'

Interstate Condensed
Type designers usually shrink the counters and correspondingly tighten the letterspacing of heavier weights in a family. Some bold fonts have slightly taller x-heights than their roman counterparts to compensate for their voluptuousness.

The idea of a family of fonts was not fully developed until well after movable type became widespread. Italic, a scriptlike, more condensed typeface style, was first introduced in Italy in 1500 as an informal face for smaller, less expensive books. Later, printers began to combine italic and regular faces on the same page, and by the seventeenth century it had become a standard practice to mix roman and italics together, often on the same line. Today, typographers use families to easily create a cohesive page, precluding the need to intermingle many unrelated fonts. Toward this end, type designers usually conceive a typeface family to function as a multifaceted system, with a variety of weights, alternates, and italics working in tandem.

A true italic font is an original design, not merely a sloped version of the regular style. Since italics are more closely related to handwriting than roman type is, designers often give their italics scriptlike characteristics, such as replacing a roman's

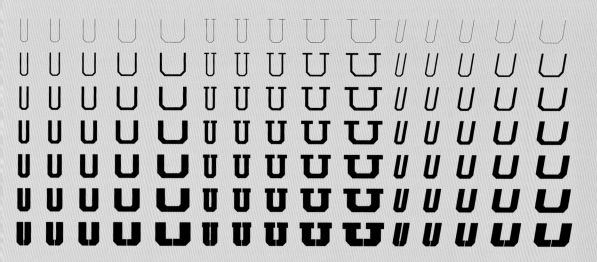

United
Type family of 105 fonts, 2006
Tal Leming, House Industries

Unlike the average human family, typeface families keep getting bigger. Some of today's megafamilies have hundreds of weights and styles, from ultra thins, inlines, and hairlines to ornaments, foreign languages, and alternate characters. Software interpolation provides shortcuts for creating intermediate weights without having to draw completely new character sets for each font.

lowercase
SMALL CAPS
UPPERCASE

Suddenly the dreaded words, SYSTEM ERROR, appeared on screen.

Suddenly the dreaded words, SYSTEM ERROR, appeared on screen.

SMALL CAPS or MID CAPS *are not just shrunken versions of regular-size capitals. Type designers draw a set of small caps separately to maintain the stroke weight, color, and width of the corresponding roman. Small caps are typically more extended and have greater letterspacing than their full-size counterparts.*

two-story a with a single-story letter. These subtle variations in drawing style often distinguish an italic more than its degree of slant. While true italics are approached as separately drawn fonts, some typefaces with a machinelike or geometric system, such as Futura or Univers, may not lend themselves to the cursive characteristics of an italic. For those, the designer may opt to draw an oblique, taking care to preserve the stroke weight, color, and curve attributes of the original roman.

Like italics, the lighter and heavier weights of a face are more than just thinned or thickened romans. Type designers compensate for a bold font's added heaviness by increasing the tapers and adding ink traps where two strokes meet. Maintaining similar curves, structure, and height ensures that additional weights speak the same language as the rest of the type family while accommodating their stylistic variations.

As the name implies, small caps are shorter versions of a typeface's capital letters. Most well-designed fonts, especially book fonts, include at least one weight of small caps similar to or slightly taller than the roman's x-height. Typographers typically use small caps for setting uppercase text within body copy, making the relationships between small caps and lowercase an important concern for type designers. Such relationships define a good type family and allow it to work together cohesively. Font family members that fight among themselves are just as dysfunctional as any feuding clan.

SPACING AND KERNING

Type designers consider the space between letters as important as the forms of the letters themselves. Like a sculptor extracting a human figure from a block of marble, a type designer sees letters in terms of counterforms and the spaces around each character. A page of text is not only black lines on a white field but also a white space punctuated by black forms. Adjusting the side bearings of each letter orchestrates this interplay between positive and negative space, ultimately defining how a font looks, feels, and works.

Spacing a font is an art unto itself. Poor spacing can ruin an exquisitely drawn typeface, while great spacing can give a lackluster font new life. The shape of a letter works in concert with its side bearings, left and right. Small alterations to a character's form can vastly improve its spacing, while a previously troublesome letter may become cooperative through careful calibration of its side bearings. A properly drawn and spaced typeface should have an even color, exhibiting no distracting gaps or heavy spots within words. Once a font has been correctly spaced, each character will fit comfortably and evenly within its surrounding negative space.

A well-spaced and -drawn font requires less kerning, the compensation required to balance unwieldy visual spaces between specific combinations of letters. Since many characters in a typeface are irregularly shaped, some letter combinations, such as AV or Ya, inevitably produce unsightly gaps. Kerning addresses these specific issues case by case. A properly spaced T and h may feel balanced next to each other, but when the T sits next to the y it creates a distracting Ty gap (shown here without kerning). Fonts generally include anywhere from several hundred to tens of thousands of kerns to rein in the worst offenders. While it is possible to go overboard, most type designers do not feel obliged to create kerning pairs for incongruous or rarely deployed combinations such as ?A.

Like drawing the characters, spacing a typeface begins incrementally with square and round letters like the H and the O. Since most Hs and Os are fairly symmetrical, these characters will typically have equal side bearings on the left and right, providing fewer variables for the initial spacing values. Once the designer feels comfortable with these characters' side bearings, he or she can set the side bearings for the rest of the case, attempting to maintain a consistent optical space between each pair of letters. Side bearings vary from character to character. Rounded characters like the o or irregular characters like the s require smaller side bearings than straight-sided characters, to visually compensate for their softness or additional open space. A typeface's system of shared attributes applies just as readily to the spacing as to the drawing. If the n's left side is similar to the r's, then by default their left side bearings should correlate.

william
johnny1

COURIER

Molière
$78,318

CONSOLAS

Typically used for applications that mingle letters and numerals, a fixed-width or monospace font keeps each character the exact same width. While no separate spacing or kerning adjustments are necessary in a monospace typeface, maintaining even color and optical spacing when all characters must occupy equal space presents a type design challenge. Wide characters such as the M and W must be condensed, while narrow characters like the i, 1, and l must be modified to fill out their space.

For more on spacing and kerning, see Designing Type by Karen Cheng (New Haven, CT: Yale University Press, 2005).

A typical starting point for the spacing process is to set a character's side bearings to approximately 50 percent of the optical width of its counter. By looking at a string of a single character typed repeatedly, a designer can decide if the spacing should be looser or tighter. Most fonts' side bearings are optically between one half and one third of the width of its average counter space. Serifs help bridge the spaces between letters, and serif typefaces often have slightly looser optical spacing than sans serif fonts. However, uniform spacing between letters' serifs is less important than the optical spacing between the main strokes of two adjoining characters.

Different fonts have different spacing requirements depending on their end use and visual characteristics. Type designers space some faces more generously to maintain legibility at small sizes, while display faces often benefit from more compact spacing.

The goal of spacing is to achieve even rhythm and color by eliminating white gaps and tight, dark areas. A designer typically begins by determining comfortable side bearings for control characters like H and O. Then strings of the control characters are tested with additional letters at various point sizes. If any problems appear, spacing, or the character itself, must be adjusted.

Without kerning, awkward gaps appear between several pairs of these characters. Punctuation and combinations of upper- and lowercase letters frequently require kerning to maintain a font's even spacing.

ROGUES GALLERY
Too-tight letterspacing causes the characters to run together, reducing legibility and creating color problems. Type spaced too loosely creates distracting gaps between letter pairs and causes words to break apart.

nnnnn   nnnnn

INITIAL SPACING *(Side bearings set to 50 percent of each counter; feels too loose)*

nnnnn   nnnnn

FINAL SPACING *(Side bearings slightly reduced)*

LOOSEY GOOSEY   **TIGHTY WHITEYS**

SCALA SANS *(More open spacing)*   VAG ROUNDED *(Very tight spacing)*

HHHHH   OOOOO   HHOHH   HOHOHO
nnnnn   ooooo   nnonn   nononon
HHDHOHODOO   HHPHPHHHPHPHH
nnpnonopoo   nnknnnnknn   nnnvnnn
HHSHH   OOSOO   HSHSHS   OSOSOS
nnsnn   oosoo   nsnsns   ososos

SOME SAMPLE SPACING STRINGS USING THE H, O, n, AND o AS CONTROL CHARACTERS.

VAULT.   VAULT.
Wanda"   Wanda"

UNKERNED TYPE   WITH KERNING

Type designers consider the space between letters as important as the forms of the letters themselves. Like a sculptor extracting a human figure

Type designers consider the space between letters as important as the forms of the letters themselves. Like

sphinx of black quartz, judge my vow. bright vixens jump; dozy fowl quack. quick wafting zephyrs vex bold jim. two driven jocks help fax my big quiz. the five boxing wizards jump quickly. jackdaws love my big sphinx of quartz. 3,164,875,209 heavy boxes perform quick jigs and waltzes. a very bad quack might jinx zippy fowls. pack my box with five dozen liquor jugs. the quick brown fox jumps over a lazy dog. doch bep, flink sexy qua vorm, zwijgt. pa's wijze lynx bezag vroom het fikse aquaduct. the jay, pig, fox, zebra, and my wolves quack! a wizard's job is to vex chumps quickly in fog. brawny gods just flocked up to quiz and vex him. the quick onyx goblin jumps over the lazy dwarf. the lazy major was fixing cupid's broken quiver. amazingly few discotheques provide jukeboxes. voyez le brick géant que j'examine près du wharf. bâchez la queue du wagon-taxi avec les pyjamas du fakir. cozy lummox gives smart squid who

sphinx of black quartz, judge my vow. bright vixens jump; dozy fowl quack. quick wafting zephyrs vex bold jim. two driven jocks help fax my big quiz. the five boxing wizards jump quickly. jackdaws love my big sphinx of quartz. 3,164,875,209 heavy boxes perform quick jigs and waltzes. a very bad quack might jinx zippy fowls. pack my box with five dozen liquor jugs. the quick brown fox jumps over a lazy dog. doch bep, flink sexy qua vorm, zwijgt. pa's wijze lynx bezag vroom het fikse aquaduct. the jay, pig, fox, zebra, and my wolves quack! a wizard's job is to vex chumps quickly in fog. brawny gods just flocked up to quiz and vex him. the quick onyx goblin jumps over the lazy dwarf. the lazy major was fixing cupid's broken quiver. amazingly few discotheques provide jukeboxes. voyez le brick géant que j'examine près du wharf. bâchez la queue du wagon-taxi avec les pyjamas du fakir. cozy lummox

sphinx of black quartz, judge my vow. bright vixens jump; dozy fowl quack. quick wafting zephyrs vex bold jim. two driven jocks help fax my big quiz. my brave ghost pled. the five boxing wizards jump quickly. jackdaws love my big sphinx of quartz. 3,164,875,209 heavy boxes perform quick jigs and waltzes. a very bad quack might jinx zippy fowls. pack my box with five dozen liquor jugs. the quick brown fox jumps over a lazy dog. doch bep, flink sexy qua vorm, zwijgt. pa's wijze lynx bezag vroom het fikse aquaduct. the jay, pig, fox, zebra, and my wolves quack! a wizard's job is to vex chumps quickly in fog. brawny gods just flocked up to quiz and vex him. the quick onyx goblin jumps over the lazy dwarf. the lazy major was fixing cupid's broken quiver. amazingly few discotheques provide jukeboxes. voyez le brick géant que j'examine près du wharf. bâchez la queue du wagon-taxi

sphinx of black quartz, judge my vow. bright vixens jump; dozy fowl quack. quick wafting zephyrs vex bold jim. two driven jocks help fax my big quiz. the five boxing wizards jump quickly. jackdaws love my big sphinx of quartz. 3,164,875,209 heavy boxes perform quick jigs and waltzes. a very bad quack might jinx zippy fowls. pack my box with five dozen liquor jugs. the quick brown fox jumps over a lazy dog. doch bep, flink sexy qua vorm, zwijgt. pa's wijze lynx bezag vroom het fikse aquaduct. the jay, pig, fox, zebra, and my wolves quack! a wizard's job is to vex chumps quickly in fog. brawny gods just flocked up to quiz and vex him. the quick onyx goblin jumps over the lazy dwarf. the lazy major was fixing cupid's broken quiver. amazingly few discotheques provide jukeboxes. voyez le brick géant que j'examine près du wharf. bâchez la queue du wagon-taxi avec les pyjamas du fakir. cozy lummox gives smart squid who

SETTING TEXT

Type designers begin using their fonts to set words and sentences as soon as enough characters and spacing information have been resolved. Setting lines of text is helpful at every stage of the process, from drawing the initial characters to incorporating punctuation to spacing and kerning. Nothing reveals a typeface's problems quicker than printed tests. The solutions to these problems, however, are not always quick and straightforward; they may require multiple rounds of revisions. To see how the complete alphabet looks in print, type designers set paragraphs of *pangrams*, sentences containing every letter of the alphabet. By using each alphabet letter with relatively equal frequency, pangrams like the familiar "quick brown fox jumps over the lazy dog" make it easy to find letters with weight problems, improper spacing, and general issues that disrupt the flow and color of the text.

So during centuries: for the first ninety years of typography printing saw the exploration and development of justified and unjustified setting, of italic, of new letters J and U surviving; some, like the omega, left at last, of punctuation marks. After, though, interest shifted toward experiment in letter design and, later, mechanical improvement. All later work, until the demands of writers such as Blake or Mallarme disrupted the conventions, considered the typographic grid unalterable. And even with the poets, their understanding of typography was such that they hardly considered the presentation of their personal desires a challenge to the grid. And here's a sadness. Typography, as taught in schools of art, and captioned in the illustrated books, is mostly but a word delimiting a field of art-/craft-history; books of types, of typographic ornaments and rules, of title pages (fewer books of double-page spreads), sit on their shelves or presses. Typographic (sic) has become the study of placing letters on a field: typography, a more precise

So during centuries: for the first ninety years of typography printing saw the exploration and development of justified and unjustified setting, of italic, of new letters J and U surviving; some, like the omega, left at last, of punctuation marks. After, though, interest shifted toward experiment in letter design and, later, mechanical improvement. All later work, until the demands of writers such as Blake or Mallarmé disrupted the conventions, considered the typographic grid unalterable. And even with the poets, their understanding of typography was such that they hardly considered the presentation of their personal desires a challenge to the grid. And here's a sadness. Typography, as taught in schools of art, and captioned in the illustrated books, is mostly but a word delimiting a field of art-/craft-history; books of types, of typographic ornaments and rules, of title pages (fewer books of double-page spreads), sit on their shelves or presses. Typographic (sic) has become the study of placing letters on a field: typography, a more precise form of lettering. And lettering, calligraphy, has died some sweet Roman death of letraset itself below the ground. It is time, after half a millennium, for the reassess-

EMPIRE STATE BUILDING

Empire State Building
Typeface, 2007
Designed with Paul Barnes

Below:
Houston
Newspaper typeface, 2003

Review

The Best Bars in America Part

Above and right:
Stag and Stag Bold Dot
Magazine display typefaces,
2005–2008

Gold

AND GINGER BEER

ANCH

to move to California

idland

in from the next county

Shortage

Right:
Farnham
Typeface, 2004

$9,532/month is almost worth it for the locat

Bohemian Neighbo

FIREPLAC

Engineer guilty in military sec
The single returns to haunt mu
Militant 'Mickey Mouse' pulle
Cheney defends extended depa
OxyContin maker, execs ple
Drug patch to treat Parkinso
Lohan plays a stripper in n
Fistfight mars Boston Pops'
Scientists directly target ca
Diet: Thin people may be fa
Britain's Blair to step dow
Blair legacy: reform, peace

surance claims down 62%

Migraine

HINGS YOU DON'T KNOW

s We Won't Be Covering This Month

nswer

Above:
Amplitude
Typeface, 2001, 2003

Left:
Stag Sans
Magazine display typeface, 2007

Above:
Publico
Newspaper typeface, 2007
Initial version designed
with Paul Barnes

INTERVIEW: CHRISTIAN SCHWARTZ

American type designer Christian Schwartz created and published his first digital font when he was fourteen years old. Since then he has designed well-known retail type families including Neutraface, Farnham, and Amplitude, along with custom typefaces for publications such as Esquire, the Guardian, *and the* Houston Chronicle.

How do you, as a contemporary type designer, work within the constraints and historical context of book/text type design? I got into type design because I love to read—magazines and newspapers as well as books. This probably explains why my taste in type skews a little conservative and explains my love of historical typefaces. Although these three kinds of media are all printed on paper, the text type for each has pretty different needs. Newspapers are usually printed in narrow columns with very little leading, while book type is typically in wide columns with generous leading, on much nicer paper, and so on. I've enjoyed working within and pushing against these constraints, and there's much more to explore.

What is the most crucial step in the development of a typeface? For me, deciding on or understanding a typeface's purpose is the most crucial step. The typefaces for the Empire State Building referenced the building's existing lettering but also had to be legible for signage, while taking into account materials and manufacturing processes. I like working with these kinds of constraints, because they usually force me to be clever and use some lateral thinking. For self-initiated projects like Amplitude and Farnham, I've come up with strict guidelines for myself, because having a problem to solve keeps me focused. Out in the wild, designers will use a typeface in unexpected ways, but it must do one thing really well before it can do other random things well.

How does your type design process start? Before I start drawing something I spend a lot of time ruminating on ideas and discussing things with my frequent collaborator, Paul Barnes. I also like to look at historical examples of how problems have been solved before—I may not follow what my predecessors did, but then at least I know what I'm disagreeing with and why.

In your opinion, what makes a good typeface? A good typeface is well crafted and useful, and sets up into attractive-looking words. It also holds together as a complete system, where individual letters don't distract the reader. A good typeface doesn't make you wonder what you might do with it, or why it exists.

What is the most important advice you received when you first began designing type? Tobias Frere-Jones told me to always space as I draw, which is obvious once you know it, but was a revelation at the time. Matthew Carter told me that I didn't need to learn calligraphy to be a good type designer, unless I wanted to. That opened up my eyes to the fact that there are many different, legitimate ways to create good typefaces.

GLOSSARY

*Terms describing the structure and features
of letters are illustrated on pages 30–32.*

ALTERNATE CHARACTERS Additional glyphs not part of a font's standard character set; typically, variants of existing letters that can be substituted at the typographer's discretion.

APERTURE The opening found in letters like a, c, e, and s.

AXIS The direction of stroke emphasis within a letter. Letters with modulated strokes display thick and thin areas, based on the angle of the writing tool used to create them.

BOOK TYPE or TEXT TYPE Typefaces designed to maintain readability and be used to set longer bodies of text such as books and periodicals.

BROAD-NIBBED PEN A flat-tipped writing tool used for most handwriting until the popularization of expandable nibs in the eighteenth century.

CHARACTER An elemental unit of written language, such as an alphabet letter.

CHARACTER SET or GLYPH SET The complete set of glyphs that make up a font or alphabet.

COLOR The overall lightness or darkness of a character, font, or page of text.

CONTRAST The amount of variation from thick to thin within and between the strokes that form a character.

COUNTER or COUNTERFORM A partially or fully enclosed area within a letter.

CURSIVE Letters with a flowing quality, often connected. (See also *italic* and *script*.)

DARK Describing characters or bodies of text with a low ratio of negative space within and around them. Can also refer to specific strokes or parts of characters.

DIACRITIC or ACCENT MARK A small, simple mark added above or below a character that generally signifies a change in pronunciation. Various languages employ different diacritics.

DISPLAY TYPE or DISPLAY LETTERING As opposed to book or text type, letters that are meant to be used at larger sizes for shorter amounts of text.

EXPANSION The thickening of a stroke caused by increased pressure on a pen that has an expandable nib.

FAMILY A group of related fonts designed to work together, such as a roman, italic, and bold weight of a single typeface.

FONT The character set of a single weight or style of a type family, although the term is often used interchangeably with *typeface*.

GLYPH A visual representation of a letter, numeral, symbol, ligature, or other distinct written, lettered, or typographic mark.

HUMANIST A writing style developed in fifteenth-century Italy that influenced early European type design. Humanist type is informed by broad-nibbed pen handwriting and usually possesses an angled axis.

INCIPIT The opening lines or page of a book, chapter, or poem. The incipit pages of medieval manuscripts are often embellished or treated distinctly from the main text.

INITIAL The first letter of a page or chapter that is larger, decorative, or otherwise called out from the body text.

INK TRAP An increased indentation that relieves some of the darkness where two strokes meet. Ink traps are often found in the diagonal joins of bold fonts.

ITALIC A style of letters derived from cursive writing that is typically more inclined and rounded than upright roman characters.

KERNING or KERNING PAIR An additional spacing adjustment that reduces cumbersome spaces between specific pairs of letters or a letter and a punctuation mark within a typeface.

LATIN ALPHABET See *roman*.

LEGIBILITY The recognizability of an individual letter; the ease with which a character is read and distinguished. (See also *readability*.)

LETTERING Characters that are built from multiple actions or strokes, as opposed to type or writing.

LETTERSPACING The amount and rhythm of space between characters in a typeface, word, or lettering treatment.

LIGHT Describing letters or text of a paler typographic color with a high ratio of negative space within and surrounding them.

LINING NUMERALS Numerals of uniform height that sit on the baseline and typically relate to the height and proportions of the capital letters of a typeface.

LOGOGRAM A single glyph that represents an entire word or combinations of phonetic sounds. The Chinese alphabet and our Arabic numerals are logographic.

MINUSCULE A lowercase letter. The term comes from medieval writing styles that were precursors to the roman lowercase alphabet.

MODULATION Variation in stroke width.

NEGATIVE SPACE or **WHITE SPACE** The space around and within a character.

OBLIQUE Sloped roman characters, as opposed to *italic*.

PHONEME The smallest unit of speech. In a phonetically based alphabet, each roman letter represents one or more sounds.

READABILITY Related to legibility, but more broadly the overall ease with which words, sentences, and larger bodies of text can be read and comprehended.

ROMAN The upper- and lowercase alphabet originally derived from ancient Rome, now widely used throughout the world. Also refers to the upright, regular weight of a typeface.

ROMAN Of classical Rome—lettering styles used in the Roman Empire.

ROTATION A change in the angle and orientation of a flat-tipped writing tool.

SANS SERIF A letter or font that lacks serifs.

SCRIPT Running cursive letters that usually join with a connecting stroke.

SERIF A short finishing line or mark at the end of a stroke.

SIDE BEARING The space on either side of character within a font.

STROKE A single mark or motion of the writing implement. When applied to type or built-up lettering, the term is more metaphorical.

TERMINAL An enlarged, rounded, or ornamental ending that completes some (typically curved) strokes on serif letters like the c, f, and r.

TEXT FIGURES or **OLD STYLE NUMERALS** Numerals with ascenders and descenders, designed to complement the proportions of the lowercase alphabet.

TITLING CAPITALS A set of capitals created explicitly for display use, generally as a companion font to a text typeface.

TRANSLATION The variation in stroke width caused by changes in stroke direction of a flat-tipped writing tool held at a relatively steady angle. (See the diagram on page 52.)

TYPE Characters that can be uniformly reproduced through a single action, as opposed to lettering or writing.

TYPEFACE A font or type family.

TYPOGRAPHER A person who works with and is knowledgeable about type. The term *type designer* more accurately describes someone who creates type.

WRITING Letters that can be quickly produced by hand with a minimal number of motions, as opposed to lettering or type.

BIBLIOGRAPHY

Andel, Jaroslav. *Avant-Garde Page Design 1900–1950.* New York: Delano Greenridge Editions, 2002.

Barnes, Paul. "The Story of the Guardian Typefaces 2003–2005." Unpublished PDF document from the designers.

Benson, John Howard, and Arthur Graham Carey. *The Elements of Lettering.* 2nd ed. New York: McGraw-Hill Book Co., 1950.

Bringhurst, Robert. *The Elements of Typographic Style.* Version 2.5. Point Roberts, WA: Hartley and Marks, 2002.

Brown, Frank Chouteau. *Letters & Lettering.* Worcester, MA: Davis Press, 1921.

Carter, Harry. *A View of Early Typography: Up to about 1600.* 1969. Reprint with minor corrections and changes, with an introduction by James Mosley. London: Hyphen Press, 2002.

Cheng, Karen. *Designing Type.* New Haven, CT: Yale University Press, 2005.

Consuegra, David. *American Type Design & Designers.* New York: Allworth Press, 2004.

Conti, Gene, Carl Lehmann, Robert Rose, and George Sohn, eds. *Photo-Lettering's One Line Manual of Styles.* New York: Photo-Lettering, Inc., 1988.

Cruz, Andy, Ken Barber, and Rich Roat. *House Industries.* Berlin: Die Gestalten Verlag, 2004.

Drucker, Johanna. *The Alphabetic Labyrinth: The Letters in History and Imagination.* New York: Thames and Hudson, 1999.

Gray, Nicolete. *A History of Lettering.* Oxford: Phaidon Press, 1986.

Hagmann, Sibylle. *Dwiggins Revisited.* Bern, Switzerland: TM, 2007.

Hoi-Yin. "Akiem Helmling Interview." *Sketchblog,* January 20, 2007, sketchblog.guava.nl/2007/01/20/akiem-helmling-interview.

Kelly, Rob Roy. *American Wood Type: 1828–1900.* New York: Da Capo Press, 1977.

Leach, Mortimer. *Lettering for Advertising.* New York: Reinhold Publishing Corp., 1956.

Lupton, Ellen. *Thinking with Type.* New York: Princeton Architectural Press, 2004.

McGrew, Mac. *American Metal Typefaces of the Twentieth Century.* 2nd rev. ed. New Castle, DE: Oak Knoll Books, 1993.

Microsoft Typography Group. *Microsoft Typography.* Redmond, WA: Microsoft Corporation, 2008, www.microsoft.com/typography.

Middendorp, Jan. *Dutch Type.* Rotterdam: 010 Publishers, 2004.

Morris, William. "Art and Its Producers." 1888. Republished from *Art and Its Producers, and The Arts and Crafts of To-day: Two Addresses Delivered before the National Association for the Advancement of Art.* 1901. William Morris Internet Archive, www.marxists.org/archive/morris.

Noordzij, Gerrit. *Letterletter: An Inconsistent Collection of Tentative Theories That Do Not Claim Any Other Authority Than That of Common Sense.* Point Roberts, WA: Hartley and Marks, 2000.

Noordzij, Gerrit. *The Stroke: Theory of Writing.* Translated by Peter Ennenson. London: Hyphen Press, 2005.

Rehe, Rolf F. "Legibility." In *Graphic Design and Reading: Explorations of an Uneasy Relationship,* edited by Gunnar Swanson. New York: Allworth Press, 2000.

Rothenstein, Julian, and Mel Gooding, eds. *ABZ: More Alphabets and Other Signs.* San Francisco: Chronicle Books, 2003.

Ryan, David. *Letter Perfect: The Art of Modernist Typography 1896–1953.* Rohnert Park, CA: Pomegranate Communications, 2001.

Smeijers, Fred. *Counter Punch.* Edited by Robin Kinross. London: Hyphen Press, 1996.

Tracy, Walter. *Letters of Credit.* Boston: David R. Godine, Publisher, 1986.

Warde, Beatrice. "The Crystal Goblet or Printing Should Be Invisible." In *Looking Closer 3: Classic Writings on Graphic Design,* edited by Michael Bierut, Jessica Helfand, Steven Heller, and Rick Poynor. With an introduction by Steven Heller and Rick Poynor. New York: Allworth Press, 1999.

Waters, Sheila. *Foundations of Calligraphy.* Greensboro, NC: John Neal Bookseller, 2006.

Wilkinson, Alec. "Man of Letters." *New Yorker,* December 5, 2005, p. 56.

Young, Doyald. *Fonts and Logos: Font Analysis, Logotype Design, Typography, Type Comparison.* With an introduction by Hermann Zapf. Sherman Oaks, CA: Delphi Press, 1999.

INDEX
PEOPLE, GROUPS, AND MOVEMENTS

EVOLUTION OF JUBILAT'S LOWERCASE g, Typeface, 2008, Joshua Darden, Darden Studio